D1230694

DIRECT FROM DEATH ROW THE SCOTTSBORO BOYS

(AN EVENING OF VAUDEVILLE AND SORROW)

BY MARK STEIN

MUSIC AND LYRICS BY
HARLEY WHITE, JR.

★

★

DRAMATISTS
PLAY SERVICE
INC.

DIRECT FROM DEATH ROW THE SCOTTSBORO BOYS was originally produced by River Stage (Frank Condon, Artistic Director) in Sacramento, California. It was directed by Bob Devin Jones. The set and lighting design were by Kale Braden; the costume design was by Nancy Pipkin; the technical director/set construction was by David Fulk; the stage manager was Irene Velasquez; the assistant stage manager was Donna Andrews; and the composer/piano player was Harley White, Jr. The cast, in alphabetical order, was as follows:

WILLIE ROBERSON, SCOTTSBORO MOTHER,
JUROR .... Sharaye Barnett

HAYWOOD PATTERSON, JUDGE HORTON,
WALTER WHITE .... Neill Brengettsey

OZIE POWELL, SCOTTSBORO MOTHER,
VICTORIA PRICE .... Tammy Denyse

LEROY WRIGHT, RUBY BATES,
SCOTTSBORO MOTHER .... Ericka Harden

CLARENCE NORRIS, JOE BRODSKY,
JUROR .... Gregory Jolivette

ANDY WRIGHT, SAMUEL LEIBOWITZ .... Jamal J. Kelly

OLEN MONTGOMERY .... Arvin Magusara

CHARLIE WEEMS, ATTORNEY GENERAL KNIGHT,
PROSECUTOR .... DeAngelo Mack

EUGENE WILLIAMS, JUROR .... Helen Terry

DIRECT FROM DEATH ROW THE SCOTTSBORO BOYS was subsequently produced at The Fountain Theatre in Los Angeles, California. It was directed by Ben Bradley. The associate producer was Yvonne Bennett. The set design was by Thomas A. Brown; the costume design was by Naila Aladin-Sanders; the lighting design was by Kathi O'Donohue; the sound design was by Kurt Thum; the prop design was by Sharon Rushing; the mask design was by April Chapman; the choreographer was Sheilagh M. Brooks; the music director was Tim Davis; the production stage manager was Alexis Miles; and the assistant stage manager was Eric Matikosh. The cast, in alphabetical order, was as follows:

LEROY WRIGHT, SCOTTSBORO MOTHER .... Erinn Anova

OZIE POWELL, SCOTTSBORO MOTHER,
RUBY BATES .... Sheilagh M. Brooks

WILLY, JOE BRODSKY .... Gilbert Glenn Brown

SKIP THE PIANO PLAYER .... Tim Davis

OLEN MONTGOMERY, GENERAL KNIGHT .... Yaphet Enge

CLARENCE, JUDGE HORTON, PROSECUTOR .... Andre Jackson

HAYWOOD PATERSON ....…....... Edwin Morrow

ANDY WRIGHT, WALTER WHITE ...….............................. Don Richardson

CHARLIE WEEMS, SAM LIEBOWITZ ....….........….... Timothy Lopez Rogers

EUGENE WILLIAMS, VICTORIA, MOTHER,
OLD VICTORIA ....….. Bernadette L. Speakes

MALE UNDERSTUDY ....…...................................... Jemal McNeill

FEMALE UNDERSTUDY ....…........................…….... Angela Martinez

CHARACTERS

All the characters in this play are to be performed by nine black actors. Female actors depict Leroy, Eugene and Ozie — enabling females to depict Victoria, Ruby and the mothers.

HAYWOOD PATTERSON, when arrested, an 18-year-old, illiterate black youth from Chattanooga.

CLARENCE NORRIS, when arrested, a 19-year-old illiterate black youth from Warm Springs, Georgia.

CHARLIE WEEMS, when arrested, a 20-year-old black man from Riverdale, Georgia. Able to read and write.

ANDY WRIGHT, when arrested, a 19-year-old black youth from Chattanooga. Able to read and write.

LEROY WRIGHT, Andy's brother, 13 when arrested.

EUGENE WILLIAMS, Leroy's friend, 13 when arrested.

OZIE POWELL, an illiterate, black 15-year-old when arrested, from rural Georgia.

OLEN MONTGOMERY, a black 18-year-old when arrested, from Monroe, Georgia, blind in one eye and nearly blind in the other, but able to read and write.

WILLIE ROBERSON, when arrested, an illiterate, black 16-year-old from Georgia. Orphaned at age two.

These nine actors also depict, in vaudeville acts:

SCOTTSBORO MOTHERS (3)

JURORS (3)

PROSECUTOR

VICTORIA PRICE

JOE BRODSKY

WALTER WHITE

SAMUEL LEIBOWITZ

RUBY BATES

JUDGE HORTON

ATTORNEY GENERAL KNIGHT

There is also a PIANO PLAYER.

SETTING

This theater, now. There is a vaudeville annunciator board, which holds the signs announcing the various acts. Trunks and crates of various sizes, some chairs, a push broom and perhaps a simple table litter the stage — all of which are to be put to use as scenery. All the props and costumes used to depict the vaudeville characters are stored in these trunks and crates.

DIRECT FROM DEATH ROW
THE SCOTTSBORO BOYS

ACT ONE

Scene 1

Bare stage. The lights come up to reveal the nine Scottsboro Boys, grouped together, blankly facing the audience. The five who come from Georgia are dressed in overalls; the four from Chattanooga are in simple but more urban attire. Some have caps. Some wear sweaters or jackets. All are poor. Haywood steps forward.

HAYWOOD. *(To the audience.)* If there's one thing I love to do it's go places. See the world, so to speak. Startin' when I was maybe fourteen. Caught my first freight. I'd heard the older kids talkin' about how you can do it. So I give it a try. All by myself, too, since ol' Andy here was too chicken.
ANDY. *(Good-natured.)* Oh, man. *(To the audience.)* *Every* time, right off the bat, he find some way to start pokin' at people!
HAYWOOD. Went to Knoxville.
ANDY. *(Still to audience.)* But don't let that bother ya. Haywood's all right.
HAYWOOD. All of two hours or so from Chattanooga. But I'll tell ya, I never felt so free in all my life as I did that afternoon walkin' down Locust Street in Knoxville. *(Others chime in: "I know that." "Oh yeah.")* A man of the world! I knew then that from here on out, anytime I wanna by God go to Knoxville, I can just up and take myself to Knoxville! *("Got that right," etc.)* Felt that day like I owned that town! Or owned myself, anyway.
CLARENCE. *(Branching off from the group.)* That wasn't why I was on the train.
HAYWOOD. Yeah, well, you got no sense of adventure, Clarence.
CLARENCE. To me, feelin' free was smellin' the farm wakin' up in the mornin', and then again at sunset.
OLEN. *(In wire-frame glasses with thick lenses; to audience.)* In other words, when he not workin'.

7

HAYWOOD. Nashville, Memphis, Atlanta — I been all those places.

CLARENCE. Or the mud squishin' up 'tween your toes as you castin' out your fishin' line.

HAYWOOD. *(Taking in his surroundings.)* Though this be my first time in [city where they're performing]. *(The others — commenting to each other on the theater and town they're in — begin to move about, exploring the stage, each eventually finding some personal space. Meanwhile …)*

CLARENCE. Easter weekends, I remember, in Warm Springs, bunch of families get together, colored folk and white, stretch a net across the river and the men would drag it through the water, then we all of us, women and kids, grab ahold and heft that net up filled with catfish and perch and eel, jumpin' and squirmin'.

OZIE. That be us, all right! Jumpin' and squirmin'! Caught in that net! Them crackers fixin' to clean us out like fish on the riverbank. Dogs sloppin' up the guts.

CHARLIE. Okay, Ozie.

OZIE. What I doin' here? I ain't no catfish!

CHARLIE. You in the net, Ozie.

OZIE. I don't even know these niggers!

ANDY. *(Privately, indicating the audience.)* Ozie, there's whites out there.

OZIE. I wuddn't in that fight! I don't know nothin' about none of this!

CHARLIE. It was a long time ago, Ozie. It's over now.

CLARENCE. My daddy was the reason I was on that train.

CHARLIE. With me it was a woman.

CLARENCE. He was half Indian. Had long straight hair down to his shoulders.

CHARLIE. Hattie Pearl Massey.

CLARENCE. Sharecropper. All that man knew was how to work. Put us in the fields soon as we could pick. And like to beat us half to death, we didn't do what he want.

CHARLIE. Hattie taught me a little how to read, how to add, subtract and multiply.

HAYWOOD. And we know how you love multiplyin' with women. *(As some of the others snicker …)*

OLEN. Shut up, Haywood.

CLARENCE. To this day I never seen that man no more.

CHARLIE. I knew I was losin' her. To this goddamn deacon of the New Hope church. The reason I was ridin' rails was that last night, standin' on a bridge where I'd gotten her to take a walk. Up high over the river, I was feelin' somethin' like I ain't *ever* known, when all of a sudden she says … *(Conveying her sense of shock:)* "Are you gonna kill me, Charlie?" *(A beat.)* Hattie Pearl Massey. She brought out the best in me … and she brought out the worst.

8

LEROY. But you didn't hurt her, Charlie! Tell 'em what you did.

CHARLIE. *(To the audience.)* I ran. I just turned from her and ran.

HAYWOOD. *(To the audience.)* We all had our reasons for bein' on that train.

WILLIE. I had the bad blood.

OLEN. These people don't know what the bad blood means, Willie.

WILLIE. I was sick … in my privates.

OLEN. You had syphilis is what you had.

WILLIE. All I knowed is my privates got swole up so's I can hardly walk for the pain. So I find a hospital and they tole me they can't treat me, on accounta I ain't from there, 'less I got the money. "What'm I s'pose to do?" I axe 'em, "Ain't anywhere I *am* from!" "Maybe you try Memphis," they tole me. "That a big city, maybe they help you there." So I get on that freight, and curl myself up in an empty car. 'Til them men come in with their guns, I never even knowed there was trouble.

HAYWOOD. I was with Andy here, and his little brother Leroy, and Leroy'd brought along Eugene. We was on our way to Memphis, too.

ANDY. Lookin' for work.

HAYWOOD. Yeah, or whatever. Ridin' ahold of an oil tanker, when these white boys come across the top, and one of 'em — maybe it was an accident, I don't know — steps on my hand. Damn near lost my hold and falled off the train! And he don't say a thing about it! So I say to him, "Excuse me … "

ANDY. He always say he said "excuse me."

HAYWOOD. I said "excuse me."

ANDY. Well if you did, it didn't come out soundin' like no excuse me.

HAYWOOD. Well then, Andy, why don't *you* tell what happened?

ANDY. *(To the audience.)* What he said was — or what *I* heard was — "Hey! Next time you want to get by, you just tell me and I let you by."

HAYWOOD. *(To the audience.)* To which the white boy says, "Nigger, I don't ask no black bastard when I want by." *(To Andy.)* Have I got that right? *(Andy nods. To the audience.)* And off they go crawlin' over the train. So I don't say nothin'. 'Cuz I don't argue with people. *(Snickers and snorts from all of the others.)* I *show* 'em. So I say to Andy here, "We don't have to take that … stuff." 'Cept I might've used another word. "We got as much right to be on this train as they do!"

OLEN. Which, technically, was no right to be on the train.

HAYWOOD. But that's still the same amount of right as they ain't got! So we go rustle up some other coloreds.

CLARENCE. Which is where Charlie and me come in.

CHARLIE. And not just us.

HAYWOOD. That's right. People talk about the nine Scottsboro Boys, but

9

some of these nine didn't know nothin' about that fight!

WILLIE. Like me! I was way in the back of that train!

OLEN. And there was over *forty* cars! I didn't know nothin' about it, either!

HAYWOOD. Then there's others, who *not* in the nine, but who *was* in the fight! Just happen not to get caught.

CHARLIE. But they out there somewhere. They know who they are.

HAYWOOD. And together, we set out to teach them white boys a lesson. Right from the start — and as far as I'm concerned, *this is the point of the whole Scottsboro thing:* that we wasn't gonna take this shit no more!

OLEN. Haywood.

HAYWOOD. I'm sorry. But I *still* get worked up about it! 'Cuz this was the point!

CHARLIE. So we head off climbin' over the train, and come upon these white boys holed up now in a gondola car.

ANDY. The kind like they carry coal in.

HAYWOOD. And we leap to it! And by and by, seein' as we was gettin' the best of 'em, them white boys turned tail and jump from the train!

CHARLIE. And it was startin' to move along pretty good too.

HAYWOOD. Oh yeah. You could see 'em, when they hit the ground — *whoomp!* — they'd tumble and keep on arollin'.

CLARENCE. 'Til it got to the point where that last one, we hold him back.

ANDY. Speed we was up to, woulda killed hisself, or damn near, had he'da jumped.

HAYWOOD. *(To the audience.)* And that was that. That there's the whole story.

CLARENCE. You wish. *(A beat.)*

ANDY. Come to find, when we pull into the next town, they got the sheriff and every farmer in the county surroundin' that train, with rifles and shotguns.

HAYWOOD. Those white boys had gone cryin' to the law in whatever place it was where they'd jumped off. And I guess some was sorta bloody. So the law called ahead and had our asses hauled off that train.

ANDY. Except for them that got away.

HAYWOOD. Yeah. And Olen and Willie here, like they said, we hadn't even *seen* 'til they roped us all together alongside the tracks. Plus there was some whites they got for hoboin'. All of 'em dressed pretty much like us — but two of 'em, it turned out, was *female*. Which was sort of unusual but, times bein' what they was … I don't think any of us paid 'em much mind, did we? *(The others concur, as …)* Mainly we was worried about the hell we gonna pay on accounta the fight.

CHARLIE. I remember the sheriff bein' all annoyed at havin' to deal with this. Cursin' about havin' to figure out how he gonna get all of us over to Scottsboro, where they had the nearest jail.

ANDY. What I remember is my brother, Leroy, keepin' right near me.

HAYWOOD. I remember bein' told "assault with intent to murder," when I ask a deputy what this was all about.

CLARENCE. Yeah and I remember thinkin', "Like you don't know what this is all about."

HAYWOOD. Turned out we *didn't* know. Did we? *(No response from any of them.)* That afternoon, they bring those two white girls by the cell where they'd put us. The sheriff and some deputies holdin' rifles with ... Olen, what they call them kind of knives?

OLEN. Bayonets.

HAYWOOD. "Which of these boys was it?" the sheriff ask the light-haired one.

CHARLIE. Victoria Price is who she turned out to be.

HAYWOOD. And she go ... *(His cracker imitation:)* "Him and him and him and him and *him.*" As if she pickin' from a box o' chocolates.

ANDY. Ain't no joke, Haywood.

HAYWOOD. You got that right.

ANDY. *(To the audience.)* Rape. Ain't nobody used the word. But ain't nobody need to, neither.

HAYWOOD. And even though the nine of us still for the most part strangers, wasn't a one had to be told what was in store for a colored man makes advances to a white woman.

CHARLIE. The dark-haired one — Ruby was her name — when they ask her which of us done it ... she don't say nothin'! Just stood there. We all just stood there — black, white, male, female — holdin' one big breath.

HAYWOOD. 'Til some deputy says, "Well if these the ones had her, stands to reason don't it these others ravished you?" *(A beat or two, then:)*

ANDY. Kinda mousey-like she says ... "I guess."

ALL NINE. *(Almost simultaneously.)*

>   CHARLIE. And we didn't do nothin' like that!
>   HAYWOOD. We never even seen those girls!
>   ANDY. We had no idea what they was talkin' about!
>   LEROY. We never touched 'em!
>   OLEN. I wuddn't even with these guys!
>   OZIE. Wait! Wait!
>   WILLIE. I didn't know what them girls talkin' about!
>   EUGENE. We did not! We did not!
>   CLARENCE. That is a *lie!* — OW!!!

(Silence. Clarence is grabbing his hand. After several moments, the others disperse to

their personal places, except Clarence, tightly holding his hand, and …)

HAYWOOD. *(To the audience.)* "Nigger," this deputy says to Clarence, after slashin' at us, to which Clarence, he go like this … *(Holds up a hand defensively.)* … and get the palm of his hand cut, I swear to you, to the bone. 'Cuz we all seen it that night. 'Cuz they don't do nothin' about it. *(Clarence now retires to his personal place, as …)* And this deputy, after he done that, say, "Nigger, you know better how to talk to a white woman." *(Olen crosses downstage to speak to the audience.)*

OLEN. What sticks in my mind — and I know this may sound silly, seein' as what all we was faced with — was the way Haywood laughed.

HAYWOOD. Oh man, you *never* gonna stop harpin' on that part, are ya?

OLEN. Word spread fast about a pack of wild niggers ravishin' two white girls down around Scottsboro. That evenin', white folk began gathering outside the jailhouse.

HAYWOOD. *(To the audience.)* It was just somethin' about his face is all. He didn't have them glasses back then, givin' him that ejucated look. Had this one eye half open all the time and the other sorta squintin'.

OLEN. *(To the audience.)* I be *blind* in that one eye! And the other was gettin' worse all the time. Hell, to this day I don't even know where on that train I was!

HAYWOOD. *(Trying, unsuccessfully, to suppress a smile.)* Yeah well, no offense but them two different eyeballs, when that crowd outside started lobbin' shouts into the jailhouse …

ANDY. "Maybe you best mosey on home to dinner now, sheriff!"

CHARLIE. "Got enough rope there, Wilbur?"

OLEN. *(Spooked.)* Don't tell me you wasn't scared too, Haywood!

HAYWOOD. *(After a moment.)* I was scared, Olen.

ANDY. "Don't make us come in there, sheriff!"

HAYWOOD. Maybe that's why I laughed, I don't know.

CLARENCE. Tell you this. When them deputies, after it turn dark, come and open up our cell …

CHARLIE. "All right, you boys, best come on with us."

CLARENCE. They turnin' us over to 'em now, I know it!

ANDY. Took us out a back door to an alley … where there was some cars.

CHARLIE. Amazin', isn't it? — when you think about it — how half-assed we protested. Goin' on out there with 'em … Gettin' into them cars …

HAYWOOD. Lot of shit we did that night — or didn't do — we ain't so proud of now.

ANDY. Then when they go to start the cars … the lights is *dead!* Is this some kinda signal? — I remember thinkin'.

CHARLIE. And then all hell breaks loose! Sheriff cursin' 'bout the crowd cuttin' the wires! Barkin' at the deputies to rush us back inside!

ANDY. Where he sets to barricadin' the doors with desks and chairs …

OLEN. And Haywood, the worse it got, the more he laughed!

HAYWOOD. I don't know, all the things everyone was rushin' around doin' … Like Leroy here, when the sheriff try to quiet the crowd by lettin' in them reporters …

LEROY. Hey, Haywood, God [damn you — !]

ANDY. *(Overlapping Leroy.)* Aw, what you gotta get goin' on that in front of the people?!

HAYWOOD. 'Cuz that's what we here for, fellas.

ANDY. They don't need to be knowin' *every detail!*

HAYWOOD. "They did it! Them there, they had them girls — I seen 'em!"

ANDY. *(To audience, arm around Leroy.)* He was *thirteen years old!*

HAYWOOD. Includin' *you,* Olen, who he pointin' at! Maybe you too blind to remember that part!

CHARLIE. I remember he protected you, Haywood.

HAYWOOD. Yeah, lotta help that was. "All of 'em had them girls but me and my brother, Andy! Oh, and our friends, Haywood and Eugene. We four just watched."

ANDY. He was a kid. He didn't know no better.

HAYWOOD. Shit. We was *all* kids.

Scene 2

"The Scottsboro Mothers"

The piano plays as one of the Scottsboro Boys places a sign on the annunciator board with the title of this scene. This is the way each vaudeville scene will be identified. The Scottsboro Mothers enter. They sing.

SCOTTSBORO MOTHERS.
   LONELINESS
   I AM YOU
   YOU ARE ME
   WE ARE TWO
   THIS LONGING
   HAS MADE ME BLUE
   SWEET CHILD
   DON'T YOU CRY.

   WE KNOW THE TRUTH
   THEY TURN THE SCREWS
   WE NEVER THOUGHT
   THEY'D TURN FOR YOU
   SO NOW WE SEE
   WE'RE ONLY THREE
   MANCHILD
   DON'T YOU CRY.

   GRAY SHADOWS
   BLOCK THE SUN
   STEAL OUR DAYS
   UNTIL THERE'S NONE
   I'M HERE FOR YOU
   I'LL SEE YOU THROUGH
   MANCHILD
   DON'T YOU CRY.

Scene 3

"The First Trial"

As a sign is placed on the annunciator board with the title of this scene, a Scottsboro Boy, holding a white half-mask, addresses us.

SCOTTSBORO BOY. One week after our arrest, trial was held in the town of Scottsboro, Alabama. The colored clergy in Chattanooga, where four of us come from, passed the plate to hire us a lawyer. A total of fifty dollar and eight cent was collected. And a white man by the name of Stephen Roddy accepted this and come on down to defend us. Mr. Roddy was known in Chattanooga for bein' willin' to represent the colored. And also for bein' a drunk. *(The Scottsboro Boy dons the white half mask — which is the way all the white characters will be represented — becoming the prosecutor.)*
PROSECUTOR. And now, ladies and gentlemen, the prosecution calls … Miss Victoria Price! *(The piano strikes up an introduction and Victoria enters. Dressed in the simple garments of the poor. But a star. She sings, hot and sassy.)*
VICTORIA.
> WHILE CHOO-CHOOIN' FROM CHATTANOOGA,
> WHERE I WAS LOOKIN' FOR WORK,
> WITHOUT EVEN A HOW-DE-DO-YA,
> THIS ONE HERE STARTS TO FLIRT.
> HE SAYS TO ME,
> STEP OUT O' YOUR STEP-INS.
> SNIP-SNAP YOUR BRASSIERE.
> LOOK HERE, WOMAN,
> THIS'LL MAKE YOU SMILE FROM EAR-TO-EAR.
>
> THAT ONE THERE PULLED A KNIFE.
> THAT ONE THERE PULLED A GUN.
> THAT ONE THERE PULLED MY LEGS WIDE.
> THAT ONE PULLED … WELL AIN'T HE HAVIN' FUN!
> STEP OUT O' YOUR STEP-INS.
> UN-BUT-BUT-BUTTON YOUR UNION SUIT.
> LOOK HERE, WOMAN,

15

THIS TRAIN RIDE GONNA MAKE YOU
REALLY ROOT-A-TOOT-TOOT!

IF YOUR HONOR PLEASE,
I'M DOWN ON MY KNEES,
ONLY ASKIN' WHAT'S DUE ME,
GIVE THESE BOYS THE HOT SEAT!
THEY SAID TO ME,
STEP OUT O' YOUR STEP-INS.
THEY PENETRATED MY PRIVATE PARTS.
LOOK HERE, YOUR HONOR,
DON'T YA, DON'T YA, DON'T YA,
DON'T YA KNOW IT BROKE MY HEARRRRRRT!

PROSECUTOR. *(Overlapping her final note, waving a pair of panties.)* And I got the step-ins! *(He tosses the panties into the air, or maybe even into the audience.)*

Scene 4

Bare stage. Andy speaks to the audience. The others loll about the stage; some do little things to make their personal space more comfortable.

ANDY. So much of what went on, I never did understand. *(Turning to the others.)* Like why'd they put Clarence and Charlie on trial together, even though the rest of us be sittin' right there? *(The others shrug. Turning again to audience.)* On the one hand, there's all this very technical legal mumbo jumbo. And on the other hand, there's our lawyer — so smashed he can barely walk straight! Soon as the first jury go off to decide on Clarence and Charlie, the judge start in on tryin' Haywood. Then when the first jury done, the judge send the second one out, bring the first one back … like it be one of them movies with everyone runnin' in and out the doors! Jury by jury, like that, they try us. And jury by jury they say what everybody know they gonna say to begin with. Guilty.

HAYWOOD. *(To the audience.)* But then we met a man named Mr. Brodsky.

ANDY. And each time the courtroom burst into cheers!

HAYWOOD. Who come on down from the Communist Party.

ANDY. And there even a band outside that play, "There Gonna Be a Hot Time in the Old Town Tonight."

OLEN. *(To the audience.)* What got me is how proud they was of the fact that we wasn't lynched!

HAYWOOD. Mr. Brodsky say to us, "We gonna raise money. And we gonna raise hell."

CLARENCE. *(To the audience.)* I liked the man from the NAACP myself.

HAYWOOD. Aw, forget that asshole.

CLARENCE. I'm just tellin' 'em I liked him! What was his name?

CHARLIE. Walter White.

HAYWOOD. *(To the audience.)* He was all talk, that man.

CLARENCE. *(To the audience.)* Yeah but he talk the truth.

HAYWOOD. What you sayin'? Mr. Brodsky lied?

CLARENCE. I'm just sayin' the colored man told the truth.

ANDY. *(To the others.)* Y'all mind if I go on with what I'm tellin' these people? *(The others react. Ain't he snippy. To the audience.)* After it all over, we was left handcuffed together in a cell. Come mornin', it be so quiet and peaceful in that little jail there in Scottsboro. *(Turning to:)* Sorta like, Clarence, you talk about the sunrise on the farm? *(Now to the audience:)* And I find myself there lyin' on the floor, listenin' to nothin' … and wishin' for that crowd to still be outside. Even wantin' to hear that band! 'Cuz everythin' felt so over now.

HAYWOOD. What I remember wishin' for was breakfast.

ANDY. Yeah, okay, Haywood.

HAYWOOD. They never did feed us the night before and they didn't that day either.

ANDY. May I finish?

HAYWOOD. Sons of bitches.

ANDY. *(To audience again.)* It was like they was all through with us.

OLEN. Which they was, Andy.

ANDY. When they come with that truck to take us off, wasn't no one come to see us go. Felt like I'd died already. And on that long ride to Kilby Prison, none of us sayin' nothin', I kept lookin' at these guys here. A bunch of who was still pretty much strangers, and some of who was friends … and one who was my brother. My little brother. And thinkin', so this be who I die with.

WILLIE. Friday, July 10th, 1931.

OLEN. That's right, Willie.

CLARENCE. That be the day.

ANDY. And thinkin', somehow now we *all* is brothers. Or is soon to be.

CHARLIE. *(Approaching, to audience:)* I'd never been in no prison before. Never even been in trouble. We pull into Kilby, what I remember thinkin' is how big it was! So many people! Like a whole other world! A locked up world. It was sorta like walkin' into a dream … in which I was bein' greeted by the people in this place and told … congratulations! You is famous. *(The others chuckle and concur.)* Which was somethin' else, 'til then, I ain't never been before.

Scene 5

"The Amazing Communisto!"

SCOTTSBORO BOY. In the early 1930s, the Communist Party turned its attention to the plight of the Negro. Black Americans, they reasoned, were ripe for revolution. Efforts were made to organize sharecroppers, but without much success. Something more dramatic was needed to make the Communist case. We were it. Ladies and gentlemen, here now to pull a rabbit out of his hat — if not nine Scottsboro Boys out of death row — the Amazing Communisto! *(Piano fanfare as Joe Brodsky, a white man who wears a coat and tie and speaks with a thick Brooklyn accent, comes downstage carrying a briefcase. The other boys hang around in their personal places and watch in a desultory way.)*

BRODSKY. Good afternoon, fellas! ... ladies and gentlemen! ... allow me to introduce myself ... *(Presto! He produces a card in his fingertips.)* Joe Brodsky, Innanational Labuh Defense. Now I know dis is a little unusual, someone such as myself appearin' before ya today, so lemme assure everyone right from de start dere is nuttin' up my sleeve. *(Shows a sleeve.)* Oops, wait a minute ... What is dis? *(He produces from his sleeve:)* A candy bar! What's dat doin' dere? *(Tossing it to a Scottsboro Boy.)* Here, you have it. Boys, I have come to Alabama wid a briefcase on my knee. Which you are free to examine. *(Handing his briefcase to the boys.)* Because dere are dose dat say our organization pulls stunts. I disagree. What dey call stunts, we call mass action targeted to expose de imperialist tyranny over de woikin' class! Have a good look at dat briefcase, boys. Anyting in dere look like a stunt to you? *(As they shake their heads no, Brodsky takes back his briefcase, showing the audience it is empty.)* What you see, ladies and gentlemen, from de Innanational Labuh Defense, is what you get. And what you get is ... *(Reaching into his briefcase and pulling out a green silk handkerchief.)* De foist organization to challenge de legality of segregated hotels and restaurants! *(Reaching in again and pulling out a yellow silk handkerchief.)* De foist organization to provide legal aid to evicted tenants, regardless of race! *(Reaching in again and pulling out a blue silk handkerchief.)* And de foimost organization to expose and fight de whites-only policies of de reactionary so-called labuh unions of de A.F. of L.! *(The boys are impressed.)* And fellas, we are prepared to take on your case, too. *(Brodsky begins pushing the handkerchiefs into his fist, as ...)* And by dat, I don't just mean to become de defense ... but to become de *offense!* To *demand* dat de state of Alabama ... set ... you ... FREE! *(On "free" he opens his fist. The handkerchiefs are gone. The boys are agog.)* Now how, you ask, are we gonna do dat? By appealin' dese unjust voidicts? Sure, we'll do dat. Tink it'll woik?

THREE OF THE BOYS. *(Simultaneously.)*

Oh yeah!   *You'll* make it work!   You can do it!

BRODSKY. Yeah? Can pigs fly? *(The boys are unsettled by that.)* Lemme ask you guys somethin'. Why do you tink you're in de tank?

TWO OTHER OF THE BOYS. *(Simultaneously.)*

'Cuz them white girls lied?   Bunch o' crackers on that jury?

BRODSKY. Naw, naw, naw, naw, naw. *(As Brodsky pulls a blue silk handkerchief from one Scottsboro Boy's pocket, and a green silk handkerchief from another's pocket …)* Now pay close attention, fellas, 'cuz I'm about to put two and two togedduh right before your eyes. *(Showing both sides of the handkerchiefs.)* De bosses of dis country are scared, see. Why are dey scared? Dey're scared because dere's a depression goin' on dat has exposed de fundamental fallacy of de capitalist dialectic. You wid me so far? *(No, but Brodsky continues. Tying the two handkerchiefs together.)* And dey're even more scared 'cuz wid de exposure of dat lie, de woikers — both black and white — are beginnin' to see dere common interests. So what do de bosses gotta do? Dey gotta smash dat solidarity. And how dey gonna do it? By executin' nine black woikers on a trumped-up charge of rapin' two white woikers! *(He holds up his linked handkerchiefs.)* Now, am I sayin' de bosses *told* dese girls to say what dey did? No. But I am sayin' de powers dat be recognize an opportunity when dey see one! I'm tellin' ya, boys, dere's more to dis case den meets de eye. Now gadder round here, 'cuz for dis particular demonstration of legerdemain, I'll need each and every one of yous to volunteer. *(The boys approach. Stretching out the linked handkerchiefs.)* You take dis end. And you take dat end. Now, all of yous join togedduh and ball dat up and hold it in de middle of all of your hands. *(As they do, Brodsky removes his coat and places it over their joined hands.)* I am now coverin' dis up wid my coat to demonstrate to you dat what happens when woikin' people join togedduh is pure magic. *(Brodsky now lifts off his coat, and the boys unfurl from their hands a bright red Soviet flag. The boys are amazed.)* How 'bout dat, huh? *(Piano plays exit music as the boys pat him on the shoulder etc.)* Thank you very much! Joe Brodsky, fellas, Innunational Labuh Defense! *(Producing a contract.)* Here's little somethin' for you guys to sign. *(As the boys flock to the contract and sign it …)* Simple representation agreement. Don't, by de way, talk wid any odduh loiyahs dat may come to see you. Okay, everyone signed? We comrades now? *(Taking the contract, waving it as he goes.)* Tanks again, folks!

Scene 6

"A Poem by Walter White"

The piano segues into a more dignified melody as Walter White crosses down-stage center. He is a highly educated black man. The Scottsboro Boys lounge in their personal places and listen.

WALTER WHITE.
    I'M NOT CERTAIN I CAN TOP THAT ACT.
    IT WAS TRULY QUITE SOMETHING TO SEE.
    I COME FROM A GROUP WITH A LITTLE MORE TACT,
    THE N-DOUBLE-A-C-P.

(The boys guffaw and dismiss this guy, so straitlaced and corny. Perseveres with his poem.)

    YES, WE'VE HEARD OF YOUR CASE,
    AND FOLLOWED YOUR TRIAL, SO CRUEL, NOT TO MENTION
        SO CRASS.
    BUT FRANKLY, THE ISSUE IS MORE ABOUT RACE
    THAN OVERTHROWING THE RULING CLASS.

(The Scottsboro Boys lose interest. One yawns.)

    I KNOW THE REDS GOT HERE FIRST, WITH THEIR LINES WELL
        REHEARSED,
    AND THEIR VISIONS OF HEAVEN ON EARTH.
    NO, THEY DON'T DILLY-DALLY; YES, THEY HOLD REAL BIG RAL-
        LIES,
    BUT THEY'RE THE DEVIL! *AND YOU WILL BE CURSED!*

(The Scottsboro Boys are startled. Walter White continues, regaining composure but gathering momentum.)

    THESE COMMUNISTS, FELLAS, WILL MAKE FOLKS HERE MAD!
    THEY'LL JUST USE YOU TO GET OTHERS TO JOIN!
    THEN WHEN THE STATE FRIES YOU, THEY'LL DEIFY YOU,
    SINCE YOUR *DEATHS* WILL *BEST* MAKE THEIR POINT!

(The boys are paying close attention now.)

    AND WHO ARE THESE COMMIES? WITH THEIR BREATH LIKE
        SALAMIS.
    HEY, IT'S JUST US NOW, SO WE CAN TALK STRAIGHT.
    EGGHEADS AND NEW YORKERS, WITH A FEW BLEEDING

HEART SORTS.

BUT THEY'RE WHITE FOLK … SO MAKE NO MISTAKE.

(Others react vocally now. "Amen." Completely the preacher now.)

NOW LET ME EXPLAIN WHAT WE CAN ARRANGE,

IF YOU'LL DISMISS THE C.P. FROM NEW YORK.

YOU'LL GET A *GOOD* LAWYER WHO'LL DO SOMETHING FOR YOU,

LIKE APPEAL TO THE SUPREME COURT!

(Two more of the boys join in. "Hallelujah." "Testify!" Imbued with the spirit.)

WE'LL WORK WITH THE PEOPLE WHO WORK WITH THE PEOPLE

WHO PULL THE STRINGS IN THIS SLEEPY OLD STATE!

("Sing out, brother!" "Praise be!" "Tell it!")

TRUE, WE DO COMPROMISE! …

("That's all right.")

… BUT YOU'LL COME OUT ALIVE!

("Lord have mercy.")

IF THE N-DOUBLE-A-C-P NAVIGATES!

(Piano fanfare as some of the Scottsboro Boys call out "Amen" and "Where do I sign?" Walter White holds out a contract. The boys flock to it. Except for Haywood — he's not sold.)

Scene 7

Bare stage. Olen reads today's paper from whatever town they're performing in. Upstage, Charlie, Andy, Eugene and Leroy quietly play cards. Haywood is selling something to Willie. Ozie is off alone. Clarence speaks to the audience.

CLARENCE. Here's how I see it. Haywood was an asshole. Kind of guy always had a little somethin' goin' on the side. Plus he had an attitude. Which is what got us into this mess in the first place. And which is why, you ask me, he dig all that Communist jazz. 'Cuz them Reds, man, you want to talk about an attitude! So Haywood, y'see, fit right in with them.

HAYWOOD. I hope you know I'm hearin' what you sayin'.

CLARENCE. I know you hearin' it!

HAYWOOD. Okay. Just so you know.

CLARENCE. *(To the audience.)* See what I mean?

HAYWOOD. Just 'cuz I don't take no shit, you call that an attitude?!

CLARENCE. I ain't talkin' to you now, Haywood! Don't you see I'm talkin' to the people?

HAYWOOD. Yeah, okay. I'll catch you later, Clarence.

CLARENCE. Yeah, right. *(Returning to audience.)* Never cared for him and I still don't. Now Charlie, on the other hand, is all right. *(Charlie gives us a wave.)* Kinda my favorite. Just a big ol' nice guy, Charlie is. Sorta quiet. That story he tell y'all 'bout thinkin' of killin' that girl on the bridge? I always found that hard to believe for Charlie. Though I suppose, you get into anyone deep enough … Ozie over there I never knew too well. Mostly kept to hisself. *(A moment, then:)* What happen with Ozie was a goddamn shame. Olen I could never figure out. Like between Joe Brodsky and Walter White, first he be with the one side, then he be with the other.

OLEN. We *all* kept switchin' back and forth.

CLARENCE. Yeah but some was leaders and some was not. Me and Charlie, maybe on accounta bein' country boys, tended to stick with the colored. Whereas Haywood and his Chattanooga pals was angrier types, so they cotton to the Reds. But Olen — maybe on accounta bein' best at readin'? — though that don't make no sense to me — was one thing one day and another the next!

OLEN. Every coin has two sides, Clarence.

CLARENCE. *(Still to audience.)* There you are. What the hell does *that* mean?!

23

HAYWOOD. *(Crossing downstage to speak to audience.)* When Mr. Brodsky come to see us, it was kinda like an angel appearin' in the middle of hell.

CHARLIE. 'Cept he was an angel who didn't believe in God.

HAYWOOD. Don't you worry about that. By then, we'da gone with anyone who was willin' just to be friendly.

ANDY. Got that right.

HAYWOOD. He tell us to call him Joe.

CHARLIE. Then that Mr. White come from the NAACP and tell us we made a horrible mistake! How the Communists just gonna use us to get people fightin'! And how the NAACP be the ones gonna save our lives. So we go with him.

ANDY. Then our mamas come and give us the dickens! Stick with the Reds, they tell us. They holdin' rallies and takin' us around the world!

OLEN. There be times, I believe, they had more Scottsboro Mothers than there was Scottsboro Boys.

HAYWOOD. Don't you worry about that, either. At least they was raisin' a ruckus.

ANDY. And the next time Mr. White come by, all he do is bad-mouth our mamas! Sayin' how they's unejucated and has been misled. That was one day, I was so proud of you, little brother. Tell 'em what you said.

LEROY. Mr. White, if you can't trust your mother, who can you trust? *(The Boys all nod at that.)*

HAYWOOD. *(Stepping forward, solemnly.)* And yet, there is a higher power. Greater even than a man's own mother.

EUGENE. Uh-oh, here come the sermon.

HAYWOOD. I refer here to the power of collective action.

EUGENE. Raise your fists and pass the ammunition!

HAYWOOD. Oh shut up, Eugene. Shit, you be the worst offender!

EUGENE. What's that s'posed to mean?

HAYWOOD. *(To the audience.)* Oh man, would you listen to him? Always playin' the innocent. You know damn well what I mean!

EUGENE. I do not!

HAYWOOD. You and Olen and Leroy and Willie …

EUGENE. Oh, man, *that?*

ANDY. Hey, let's not be jumpin' ahead now to that.

HAYWOOD. *(To the audience.)* Not *two weeks* after the four of them's released — !

OLEN. *(To the audience.)* It was a mistake.

HAYWOOD. A mistake?

ANDY. Fellas, we gettin' the story outa order here.

HAYWOOD. Tell me somethin', Olen. When the State of Alabama say to you *after six years in prison*, "Why we're sorry, it was a mistake" — what you think about that?!

CHARLIE. *(To the audience.)* Which they did — but without the apology.

HAYWOOD. *(To the audience.)* The five of us *still* inside — and them four don't lose a step lookin' after their own ass, no matter how it fucks us up!

LEROY. You do enough to fuck *yourself* up!

WILLIE.   EUGENE.

Yeah, Haywood!   That's right!

ANDY. Guys, no one's gonna know what we're talking [about here —]

HAYWOOD. *(Overlapping.)* I never joined no goddamn *vaudeville show!* (Silence. *It's out of the bag now.)* Didn't see me onstage at the Apollo Theatre! *(A beat, then:)* Walking around town sportin' *canes,* for God's sake!? I kept my dignity.

CHARLIE. 'Bout the only thing we could keep.

HAYWOOD. So go on, Eugene! How 'bout maybe a little tap dance for the audience? *(Eugene says nothing.)* Or *you,* Olen! Mr. Intellectual! Or Leroy, or Willie! Explain to the people what you think it means to … *hang* together. *(They say nothing.)* Sometimes I think we never learn.

Scene 8

"Encore!"

Same piano fanfare, as in Scene 5, as Brodsky returns to the stage.

BRODSKY. Thank you! Good to be back! How's everybody doin'? *(A beat. The Scottsboro Boys, still gloomy from the previous scene, just shrug. To the audience.)* How do you like dese guys? No sooner do I leave de stage, de NAACP comes on wid its little act — and like dat, dey sign wid 'em! *(The Scottsboro Boys react guiltily.)* Hey, you're young, don't worry about it. What do you say to one more trick? *(The Scottsboro Boys begin to perk up.)* Just holds this up right over here, if you would. *(Two Scottsboro Boys stand on crates or chairs and hold up a curtain rod with a center-slit curtain attached. The others approach, inspecting it, front and back. [Some stay in back.] To the audience.)* Ladies and gentlemen, you have hoid de NAACP say dat de Communist Party would radduh see de Scottsboro Boys die. Dis, ladies and gentlemen, is a lie. And it is a lie dat hoits. Because I too, dough a lotta people would like you to tink odduhwise, am also a human being. Accoiding to de NAACP, de proof of dere sincerity is dat dey are gonna get dese boys a *good* loiyuh. Which, as an attoiney, I find a little insultin', but okay. *(To the two Scottsboro Boys.)* Gentlemen, open de coiton, if you would. *(The two Scottsboro Boys part the curtain and a white man in a three-piece suit now appears there: Samuel Leibowitz.)* Ladies and gentlemen, say hello to Samuel Leibowitz. Know who he is? Only de best defense attoiney since Clarence Darrow. Not once has he lost a client to de death penalty! Why de guy's battin' a tousand. He's so good, he's even represented Al Capone. And Leibowitz ain't no Commie, eider. He is a one-hundred percent so-called Democrat. But I don't hold dat against him, 'cuz he has consented to represent dese boys — probably for de publicity, but I don't hold dat against him eider — since he's doin' it free of charge! Let's see de N-double-A-C-P top dat! *(Privately:)* I'll be a little honest wid ya here. Obviously, Leibowitz and de Innanational Labuh Defense don't exactly see eye to eye. But wid him we got de NAACP by de provoibial balls. 'Cuz dey, bein' collaborators wid de capitalist system, don't want a New York Jew defendin' a bunch of schvartzes in an Alabama court. God forbid dey might offend someone. But dis man, even dough he does go to shul on Rosh Hashana and still believes in dat malarkey, is — and comin' from me, I tink you'll appreciate dis — a genuine courtroom magician. But don't just take my woid for it. *(To the two Scottsboro Boys.)* If you would close the coitain, please. *(The two*

Scottsboro Boys close the curtain.) Ladies and gentlemen, I give to you ... *(Piano fanfare as the curtain is again opened and now the three Scottsboro Mothers appear there in overcoats and hats.)* ... de Scottsboro muddahs! How about that!

THE THREE MOTHERS. *(After one starts, the next joins in.)*
Haywood, you stick with the ILD! ...

You listen to me, Clarence! ...

Olen, don't you be talkin' to them other people!

BRODSKY. Ladies and gentlemen, de Scottsboro Muddahs will be appearin' in rallies all over America ... and throughout de woild!

THE THREE MOTHERS.
Haywood, they takin' me to Harlem!

Gonna be going to Boston, Chicago ...

San Francisco here I come!

BRODSKY. Plus London! ... Paris! ... Rome! ... Moscow! ...

MOTHER #1. Say what?

BRODSKY. ... and Washington, D.C.! Onstage at the Supreme Court! *(Piano plays lively exit music, as ...)*

MOTHER #1. Not in the winter I ain't goin' to no Moscow.

BRODSKY. *(Waving to the audience.)* C'mon, ladies, let's pack your bags!

Scene 9

"Victoria and Ruby"

A Scottsboro Boy sets a chair downstage center, then addresses the audience.

A SCOTTSBORO BOY. Bear with us now as we bring to the stage a unique little duo from Huntsville, Alabama. These two young ladies have put together an act that's been killing folks down there for years. Ladies and gentlemen, the women you've been waiting for … Victoria and Ruby! *(Upbeat piano music plays as Victoria, costumed as before, crosses downstage carrying in her arms her friend Ruby, also a young poor white woman. Victoria sits in the chair and holds Ruby on her lap, like a ventriloquist's dummy.)*
VICTORIA. Say Ruby, ain't ya gonna say hello to all the folks out there? *(Ruby woodenly looks out, sees the audience, and is startled.)* Aw, what's the matter, you shy? *(Ruby nods.)* Shucks, honey, they all came out here to see you and me! Now there's somethin' don't happen every day. *(Winks and wiggles her fingers at someone in the audience.)* How's about we tell 'em the one about the nine nigras and the two white girls?
RUBY. They got prostituted for rape?
VICTORIA. *(Big stage laugh.)* HA HA! Get a load of her! The word is *pro-se-cu-ted*, Ruby. "Prostituted for rape." *(To the audience.)* She's a nice girl, folks, but she's ain't got a whole lot stashed in the attic, if you know what I mean. Fact is, Ruby and me grew up on the poor side of Huntsville. *(Tearjerk piano music accompanies this.)* Ain't neither of us ever had a daddy 'round the house. So early on we hadda help support our families, workin' at the cotton mill when we could.
RUBY. And workin' the men when we couldn't.
VICTORIA. Ruby!
RUBY. What?
VICTORIA. Wasn't that way at all!
RUBY. It wasn't?
VICTORIA. *(To the audience.)* See, now there's one of the things about this case that burns me up! The way we was called hookers. Hell, maybe we had a boyfriend or two. But what's wrong with that? And o' course they gonna take care o' you. People get so technical sometimes! Drives me crazy. *(Trying to get back on track.)* Now I forgot where I was.

28

RUBY. The colored side of Huntsville.

VICTORIA. Oh will you hush?!

RUBY. What I say this time?

VICTORIA. *(To the audience.)* Fact is, folks, we did live in the same neighborhood. But we wasn't the only ones! Which brings up somethin' I don't understand. People up north say we're prejudiced. Yet here we are, me and Ruby, livin' with 'em, knowin' 'em by name …

RUBY. Even sleepin' together sometimes.

VICTORIA. Yeah, okay, you don't have to get into that.

RUBY. Oops.

VICTORIA. *(To the audience.)* But awright, long as the cat's outa the bag, maybe we have had relations with a colored fella or two. So then why — I ask you this — would I falsely accuse them boys if'n I'm just some whore who'll do it with darkies at the drop of a hat?

RUBY. To avoid prosecution under the Mann Act?

VICTORIA. Would you shut up!?

RUBY. Well it sure *looked* like we mighta been crossin' state lines for the purpose of prosti —

VICTORIA. *(Teeth clenched.)* That wasn't why I accused them.

RUBY. Why did you?

VICTORIA. Why did I? Why do you think?

RUBY. *(Thinks; guesses:)* 'Cuzza all the attention we was gettin' after they stopped the train?

VICTORIA. *(Can't help but cackle.)* Sure shocked the shit outa them hayseeds, didn't it? Findin' two girls mixed in with them hobos, most of 'em black. "Are you young ladies all right?" they asked, all gathered 'round, eyein' our titties in those overalls we was in. *(Ruby cackles, too.)* "They didn't do nothin' to you young ladies, now did they?"

RUBY. I could see Victoria here was eatin' this up. First time in her life, she was bein' treated like a southern belle.

VICTORIA. Just what, pray tell, does that mean?

RUBY. What I say this time?

VICTORIA. Damn you, Ruby, can't you stick to the script?

RUBY. I'm sorry.

VICTORIA. Cheezus. Where was I?

RUBY. Makin' up the shit you told the sheriff.

VICTORIA. Ruby!

RUBY. *(Flustered.)* I mean — ! I mean — ! You were yellin' at me about stickin' to the script.

VICTORIA. No, not now! *Then!*

RUBY. I meant then. Remember?

VICTORIA. Oh boy. Would you just let me do the talking?

RUBY. Oh! Okay, that part! You told me to let *you* do the talking.

VICTORIA. Ruby, for God's sake!

RUBY. Oh, *that* part?

VICTORIA. *(Dizzy.)* What part?

RUBY. Where you said, "Ruby, for God's sake, *five plus four is nine.*" *(To the audience.)* So all I'd have to remember, she said, was *four* of 'em.

VICTORIA. I give up. Hit it, Skip. *(Or whatever the piano player's name is. The piano player commences to play "Dixie" as …)*

RUBY. But I couldn't keep 'em straight. So at the trial I just said a bunch had her and the rest had me.

VICTORIA. *(Hauling Ruby away.)* Good night, folks!

RUBY. *(Being hauled off by Victoria.)* The *first* trial, that is. But at the *second* trial … *(To Victoria.)* Hey! I'm just gettin' to the good stuff!

30

Scene 10

"Judge James Horton"

SCOTTSBORO BOY. After the first trials in Scottsboro, Mr. Leibowitz appealed to the Alabama Supreme Court and then went on up to the United States Supreme Court. Up there, they ordered the case retried based on the lack of due process and of competent defense counsel. The second trial, as part of that due process, was moved to Decatur, Alabama. Ladies and gentlemen, coming to you from his courtroom in Decatur, Judge James Edwin Horton! *(Starts off, then stops.)* Oh. By the way, everything he's about to say ... is quotes. *(Judge Horton enters, in his judicial robe.)*

JUDGE HORTON. Since certain matters have been brought to my attention, let me just say this. Any man, or group of men, who would engage in any act that could cause the death of the defendants or of defense counsel had best be prepared to *forfeit his life*. The National Guard that, as I speak, has surrounded this building is charged with the duty to protect these individuals and, if need be, will shoot to kill. Our civilization depends on justice. And justice, for better or for worse, depends on law. All right, let's bring back the jury.

Scene 11

"The Second Trial"

Three white jurors enter and take seats; Victoria enters and takes a seat at the witness stand; Leibowitz and Knight enter and are seated. Judge Horton, seated, presides. The Scottsboro Boy who has placed the scene's sign on the annunciator board addresses the audience.

SCOTTSBORO BOY. *(To audience, raising his right hand.)* I do solemnly swear that the testimony you are about to hear is the truth ... or part of the truth ... or not even close to the truth. *But it was said.* By the witnesses or by the lawyers. Check the record if you wanna. *(To Horton.)* Okay, judge, take it away.

JUDGE HORTON. Mr. Attorney General, you may continue.

ATTORNEY GENERAL KNIGHT. *(Stands.)* Your honor, the State has no more questions for Miss Price.

JUDGE HORTON. Mr. Leibowitz? *(Leibowitz stands and crosses casually to Victoria.)*

LEIBOWITZ. How do you do, Miss Price?

VICTORIA. *(Very wary.)* Fine, I reckon.

LEIBOWITZ. By the way, is it Miss Price or *Mrs.* Price?

VICTORIA. *(After a moment.)* Mrs.

LEIBOWITZ. Ah. What does Mr. Price do for a living?

VICTORIA. I wouldn't know.

LEIBOWITZ. I see. What do *you* do for a living, Mrs. Price?

VICTORIA. Work at the cotton mill.

LEIBOWITZ. Do you work there now?

VICTORIA. There's lay-offs now.

LEIBOWITZ. Well then what do you do now?

VICTORIA. *(Pointedly.)* The best I can.

LEIBOWITZ. Say, do you still live in Huntsville, Mrs. Price?

VICTORIA. Yeah.

LEIBOWITZ. Nice town, Huntsville.

VICTORIA. I think so.

LEIBOWITZ. Ever know a man there by the name of Lester Carter?

VICTORIA. *(After a moment.)* Who?

LEIBOWITZ. Oh, I was under the impression you were introduced to him by Jack Tiller when you and Jack were in the city jail for adultery and fornica —

KNIGHT. Objection, your honor.

JUDGE HORTON. Sustained.

LEIBOWITZ. Mrs. Price, you were visiting Chattanooga on the weekend in question, is that right?

VICTORIA. I was lookin' for a job.

LEIBOWITZ. You like Chattanooga?

VICTORIA. It's all right.

LEIBOWITZ. Go there often?

VICTORIA. Sometimes.

LEIBOWITZ. Sometimes you go often?

VICTORIA. I go sometimes.

LEIBOWITZ. I see. Where did you stay on the weekend in question?

VICTORIA. At the boarding house of Mrs. Callie Brochie.

LEIBOWITZ. Which is where, Mrs. Price?

VICTORIA. Seventh Street.

LEIBOWITZ. Do you often stay at Mrs. Brochie's?

VICTORIA. Sometimes.

LEIBOWITZ. How long would you say you've known Mrs. Brochie?

VICTORIA. A while.

LEIBOWITZ. (Suddenly hot.) HOW LONG?

VICTORIA. (Startled.) Couple years.

LEIBOWITZ. (Suddenly friendly.) Say, I wonder if I might ask you, Mrs. Price, if you're sure the name Lester Carter doesn't ring a bell?

VICTORIA. I don't remember.

LEIBOWITZ. Do you remember the penalty for perjury?

KNIGHT. Objection!

LEIBOWITZ. Can you read and write, Mrs. Price?

KNIGHT. Your honor!

VICTORIA. 'Course I can!

LEIBOWITZ. Ever read magazines like, say, *The Saturday Evening Post*?

KNIGHT. Oh now really, Mr. Leibo —

LEIBOWITZ. ARE YOU AWARE THAT THE MUNICIPAL RECORDS OF CHATTANOOGA SHOW ABSOLUTELY *NO ONE* BY THE NAME OF CALLIE BROCHIE FOR THE LAST TEN YEARS? THAT THERE ARE *ABSOLUTELY NO BOARDING HOUSES* ON, OR EVEN NEAR, SEVENTH STREET IN CHATTANOOGA? THAT THE NAME CALLIE BROCHIE IS, IN FACT, THE *EXACT* NAME OF THE HEROINE IN A

ROMANTIC SERIAL PUBLISHED TWO YEARS AGO IN *THE SATUR-DAY EVENING POST*?!

VICTORIA. I don't remember!

LEIBOWITZ. WHERE DID YOU STAY IN CHATTANOOGA?

VICTORIA. I don't remember!

LEIBOWITZ. WAS IT AT A HOBO JUNGLE?

VICTORIA. I DON'T REMEMBER!

LEIBOWITZ. DO YOU KNOW LESTER CARTER?

VICTORIA. NO! *(A beat, then:)* Or maybe I met him once, I don't know. *(A beat.)*

LEIBOWITZ. *(Mr. Nice Guy.)* So, as I understand it, you and Ruby Bates were riding in a gondola car located next to a box car?

VICTORIA. That's right.

LEIBOWITZ. And the defendants came leaping down into the gondola car from on top of the box car?

VICTORIA. Yup.

LEIBOWITZ. Maybe you can clear something up for me, Mrs. Price. How do you explain the fact that the gondola car in which the deputies found your snuff box was located five cars away from the nearest box car?

VICTORIA. I don't know. Maybe someone put it there.

LEIBOWITZ. Well tell me this, do you recall if there was cargo in the gondola car?

VICTORIA. There was chert.

LEIBOWITZ. Which is hard chunks of rock?

VICTORIA. That's right.

LEIBOWITZ. Must've been terribly painful, five burly young men forcing you down and assaulting you on those rocks.

VICTORIA. It certainly was.

LEIBOWITZ. I assume you struggled.

VICTORIA. You bet I did!

LEIBOWITZ. Got your back all cut up and bruised?

VICTORIA. Sure did.

LEIBOWITZ. Curious the doctor didn't find any cuts or bruises on your back.

VICTORIA. *(Caught, but only momentarily.)* I wouldn't know.

LEIBOWITZ. I'll ask you directly, Mrs. Price. Why were there no cuts or bruises on your back?

VICTORIA. I don't know, I can't see my back!

LEIBOWITZ. In fact, the physician found virtually no scrapes or bruises *any-where* on your body, did he?

VICTORIA. I don't know!

LEIBOWITZ. Shall I have the court reporter read you his testimony?

KNIGHT. Objection.

JUDGE HORTON. Sustained.

LEIBOWITZ. Mrs. Price, would you be good enough to tell this jury what the Mann Act is?

KNIGHT. Objection.

JUDGE HORTON. Sustained.

LEIBOWITZ. Have you ever been arrested for prostitution, Mrs. Price?

KNIGHT. Objection.

JUDGE HORTON. Sustained.

LEIBOWITZ. Mrs. Price, how do you explain the fact that following your claim that five young men had just had sexual relations with you, the doctor had to insert a swab all the way to your cervix to obtain enough semen for a microscopic slide?

KNIGHT. *(Shocked.)* Mr. Leibowitz!

JUDGE HORTON. Sustained.

LEIBOWITZ. Are you aware, Mrs. Price, that the average life span of spermatozoa in the vagina is over twenty-four hours?

KNIGHT. Objection.

JUDGE HORTON. Sustained.

LEIBOWITZ. Yet not *two* hours after your alleged attack, what few sperm the doctor did find were all dead.

KNIGHT. Objection.

JUDGE HORTON. Overruled.

KNIGHT. *(Startled.)* But your honor!

LEIBOWITZ. *Dead,* Mrs. Price! Meaning one day old *at the least!* How do you explain that?

VICTORIA. I don't explain it!

LEIBOWITZ. No stains on your clothing. No dried patches of semen on your skin. No cuts, no scrapes, no bruises! Just a couple drops of old, *dead* sperm! *Any* explanation, Mrs. Price?

VICTORIA. I ain't got as much ejucation as you!

LEIBOWITZ. I'm finished with this witness. *(Victoria stares bullets at Leibowitz, then gets up and leaves the stand.)*

KNIGHT. Your honor, the prosecution rests.

JUDGE HORTON. Mr. Leibowitz?

LEIBOWITZ. The defense calls Miss Ruby Bates. *(Ruby enters, now dressed in stylish clothes and a feathered hat. Passing Victoria, she has to endure a scorching look.)*

KNIGHT. Your honor, I object! For three weeks, we have been searching for this witness. And during that time, Mr. Leibowitz repeatedly denied knowing her whereabouts!

LEIBOWITZ. She has just this day resurfaced here in Alabama.

KNIGHT. Oh, sure.

JUDGE HORTON. Seems to me, some of your witnesses, Mr. Knight, have conveniently appeared and disappeared, too. Let's just proceed.

LEIBOWITZ. Ruby, have you ever seen me before?

RUBY. No sir.

LEIBOWITZ. Have we ever spoken to each other on the telephone?

RUBY. No sir.

LEIBOWITZ. Corresponded or communicated in any way?

RUBY. No sir.

LEIBOWITZ. Who's Lester Carter?

RUBY. He's a boy I know.

LEIBOWITZ. Did Lester Carter accompany you and Victoria Price to Chattanooga on the weekend in question?

RUBY. Yes sir.

LEIBOWITZ. Where did the three of you stay in Chattanooga?

RUBY. In a hobo jungle down near the rail yard.

LEIBOWITZ. Before your return trip on the freight train, did you engage in sexual relations with Lester Carter?

RUBY. Yes sir.

LEIBOWITZ. During that time, did you see Victoria Price engage in sexual relations?

RUBY. Yes sir.

LEIBOWITZ. With whom?

RUBY. Orville Gilley.

LEIBOWITZ. Orville Gilley? Isn't that the young fella the defendants saved from jumping off the train when it got up to speed?

RUBY. Yes sir.

LEIBOWITZ. You wouldn't know where Mr. Gilley is now, would you?

RUBY. No sir.

LEIBOWITZ. How about you, Mr. Knight?

KNIGHT. Me? No.

LEIBOWITZ. Ruby, did you see the fight on that freight train?

RUBY. No sir. We heard it. Then Orville and Lester climbed over some cars to see what all the ruckus was about.

LEIBOWITZ. Well then, Ruby, when was the first time you saw the defendants?

RUBY. After the deputies stopped the train. 'Bout an hour later maybe.

LEIBOWITZ. Are you telling this court the defendants in this case did not rape

36

you?

RUBY. That's right.

LEIBOWITZ. Did they have intercourse with you?

RUBY. No.

LEIBOWITZ. Did they touch you in any way?

RUBY. No.

LEIBOWITZ. Prior to their arrest, had they even so much as spoken to you?

RUBY. No.

LEIBOWITZ. To your knowledge, did the defendants rape, have sexual intercourse with, touch, or prior to their arrest, so much as speak to Victoria Price?

RUBY. No.

LEIBOWITZ. Ruby, what you have said here today has taken tremendous courage. I have no further questions. *(Leibowitz returns to his location. Knight approaches Ruby.)*

KNIGHT. Ruby, where were you born?

RUBY. Huntsville.

KNIGHT. Where do you live now?

RUBY. New York City.

KNIGHT. I see. You *recently* moved to New York City?

RUBY. Yes sir.

KNIGHT. That's a very pretty dress you have on today, Ruby.

RUBY. Thank you.

KNIGHT. You get that dress in New York City?

LEIBOWITZ. Objection. Irrelevant.

JUDGE HORTON. Sustained.

KNIGHT. Ruby, do you have a job?

RUBY. Not right now.

KNIGHT. Well where'd you get the money for your stylish outfit?

LEIBOWITZ. Same objection.

KNIGHT. I wish to bring out the bias of this witness.

JUDGE HORTON. *(Considers a moment, then:)* Objection overruled.

KNIGHT. Who gave you the money, Ruby?

RUBY. *(Hesitates, then:)* Mrs. Greenberg.

KNIGHT. Mrs. *Greenberg,* did you say?

RUBY. Yes sir.

KNIGHT. Is Mrs. Greenberg a member of the Communist Party?

LEIBOWITZ. Objection!

JUDGE HORTON. Sustained.

KNIGHT. Where you staying while you're down here, Ruby?

RUBY. The Cornelian Arms.

KNIGHT. Well now that's a very fine establishment. Who's footing the bill?

RUBY. I don't know.

KNIGHT. You don't know?

RUBY. I don't fully remember her name. Lillian somethin'.

KNIGHT. Cohen, Schwartz, Shapiro — something like that?

LEIBOWITZ. Objection!

KNIGHT. Did this person, whatever her name is, pay for your train ticket, too?

RUBY. I came by car.

KNIGHT. Oh, you drive a car now, do you?

RUBY. No. We were driven.

KNIGHT. Who by?

RUBY. I don't know. Some men.

KNIGHT. But you don't remember their names either?

RUBY. No.

KNIGHT. You do remember *your* name, don't you?

RUBY. Of course.

KNIGHT. Bates, right? B.A.T.E.S.?

RUBY. That's right.

KNIGHT. Just wanted to be sure you hadn't changed it to Batesberger or Batesinsky …

LEIBOWITZ. Move for a mistrial! Your honor, that kind of question —

KNIGHT. That kind of question, your honor, is, I submit, *exactly* the question! Mr. Leibowitz has defended these nine … *things* — I won't dignify them with the name of nigra, 'cuz I have known and respect nigras — by claiming their accusers are whores. 'Course, bein' the defense, he isn't obligated to prove that — but even if he did, no woman, no matter what her station in life, should have to suffer the degradation of rape. However, since he's raised the issue of whores, I say to this jury, *there is your whore! (Pointing at Ruby.)* In her silk stockings and Park Avenue hat! You didn't see Victoria Price come in here with clothes like that on her back. All she had was her shame. For which she was made to endure further humiliation from our distinguished visiting defense counsel. Maybe I'm missing something here, gentlemen, but seems to me the question is this. ARE WE GONNA LET ALABAMA JUSTICE BE BOUGHT AND SOLD BY JEW MONEY FROM NEW YORK?!

THE THREE JURORS. *(One by one.)*

No!

No!

No!

38

KNIGHT. OKAY THEN, WHADDYA SAY?
THE THREE JURORS. *(One by one.)*
Guilty!
     Guilty!
          Guilty!
KNIGHT. AND THE PUNISHMENT SHALL BE...?
THE THREE JURORS. *(Simultaneously.) DEATH!!!*

Scene 12

"Ruby"

Ruby stands alone, center stage. She sings.

RUBY.
    MY INTENTIONS HERE WERE GOOD.
    BUT I FEEL I'VE BEEN MISUNDERSTOOD.
    FOR WHEN YOU CHANGE YOUR WORD
    TRUTH CANNOT BE HEARD.
    AND IF YOU SPEAK YOUR MIND
    PEACE IS ALL YOU FIND
    I CAN'T DENY
    I LIED.
    I LIED.
    I LIED.

Scene 13

Bare stage. Haywood speaks to the audience.

HAYWOOD. Durin' the second trial, the National Guards was offerin' to give us cigarettes, and whiskey even, if'n we would sing 'em a song. Figured all darkies got good voices, I guess. *(Some of the Scottsboro Boys — not Eugene — quietly begin jamming, giving the lie to the notion that all darkies got good voices. As they try to get it right …)* So what the hell, we did. Me included. 'Cuz I considered that singin' we did together an important part of our solidarity.

ANDY. Shit, you just did it for the whiskey, Haywood.

HAYWOOD. Yeah, well, that helped. Eugene here was our lead singer, on accounta he really *did* have a voice. *(To Eugene.)* Go on, show 'em what you can do.

EUGENE. No.

HAYWOOD. Oh c'mon now, Gene! Just a little!

EUGENE. I said no. *(The jamming peters out.)*

HAYWOOD. Fact is, after that second trial, we thought this time for sure our lives be over.

ANDY. Figured if Mr. Leibowitz, with the evidence he had, couldn't convince a jury, seemed like nothin' would.

HAYWOOD. Still, he promised to fight on. And Mr. Brodsky did, too.

CHARLIE. 'Cept most of the fightin' we saw was between the two of them.

ANDY. Can say that again. Man, they hated each other!

CHARLIE. Didn't exactly fill us with confidence, hearin' about their hagglin', while we be waitin' on death row. Nothin' to do all day but chat with the neighbors, who'd move in from time to time. Then watch each one, as his day come, get led — or if need be dragged — down to the room with the big steel door.

CLARENCE. Waitin' for the buzz.

ANDY. And the lights to dim. *(A moment.)*

HAYWOOD. On the other hand, life in prison wasn't *all* bad.

OLEN. It was bad enough, Haywood.

HAYWOOD. *(To the audience.)* Yeah but, truth be told, if you got the cash, ain't nothin' you can't get yourself in there. And those days, far as cash is concerned, we was in the clover!

CLARENCE. He right about that.

HAYWOOD. People was writin' us letters and enclosin' dollar bills! And the

41

ILD was spottin' us eight bucks a month so's we wouldn't jump ship to the NAACP! *(To the others.)* I don't think there was one of us — was there? — ate prison food.

CLARENCE. Three bucks a week, you get the cook send you the same chow he do for the warden.

HAYWOOD. Hell, we was doin' better *in* jail, than we could ever hoped to have done on the outside!

ANDY. You forgettin' a lot of shit, Haywood.

EUGENE. My cell daddy always tellin' me to sing.

HAYWOOD. Yeah, okay, Eugene, let's not be gettin' into that. Could be young folk out there.

OLEN. Wait a minute. We can talk about rapin' women but not what gets done to boys in prison? Why you want to avoid that, Haywood?

HAYWOOD. I'm just sayin' there be plenty other shit we can discuss! Like when Clarence lost half a finger? Or when Charlie, workin' in the weavin' room, got his throat cut and chest rip open when a guard come at him with a bailin' hook?

EUGENE. *(Crossing downstage.)* He liked the way I sing. And so I do.

CLARENCE. *(Uneasy, hearing Eugene.)* Yeah and we knew what that weavin' room was about, too! *(To the audience.)* Puttin' labels on those clothes we make from companies some of you alls probably got on your back right now!

EUGENE. 'Cuz I know what he do to me if I don't.

HAYWOOD. Let's not be gettin' into that, Eugene!

CHARLIE. *(Also uneasy about Eugene.)* Yeah, same deal in the cannery.

EUGENE. Know what I do while I'm singin'? I go home. I make my song take me to Chattanooga.

HAYWOOD. Dammit, Eugene, don't be talkin' about it!

ANDY. Why shouldn't he? You talkin' all the time about our so-called solidarity! Who of us protected him?

EUGENE. My sister open the door, and she see me. And I smile. And she scream! *(In pain.)* AHHHH!

CHARLIE. *(Aware of Eugene's pain.)* Those guards with their whips — they'll tell you it on accounta they don't want no firearms on the inside.

EUGENE. *(Hurting.)* OOOH! OH GOD, WHERE'S MAMA?!

CHARLIE. *(Trying to distract himself.)* You ask me, State of Alabama had itself a good ol' fashion plantation goin', long after the Civil War s'posed to be over.

EUGENE. Oh Mama! Oh Mama!

HAYWOOD. *(A plea.)* Try not to be thinkin' on that, Eugene.

EUGENE. *(Tortured.)* I be thinkin' about breakfast! I be thinkin' about this big breakfast my mama gonna make me! Oh God, I make myself think about that!

Oh *Mama! MAMA! (Then, the pain abating.)* Oh God, I promise I won't never ride no freight no more, Mama. Just lemme be home again. Lemme be home. Just lemme be home. *(A pause. Andy goes to Eugene.)*

HAYWOOD. After the second trial, that Judge Horton that we had took a look at all the evidence.

EUGENE. "My little lamb," he say to me when he through, "sound so beautiful when you sing."

HAYWOOD. And he review the testimony of all the witnesses.

EUGENE. "Sing that first one again," he'd say.

HAYWOOD. And two months later, *he threw out the conviction.*

CHARLIE. Ain't no one was ready for that!

EUGENE. I ain't singing no more. *(Andy comforts Eugene.)*

HAYWOOD. He balled up the verdict … and just tossed it out!

OLEN. And next election, the voters tossed *him* out, too.

CLARENCE. Yeah. Same time that Attorney General get hisself elected Lieutenant Governor!

EUGENE. I ain't ever gonna sing no more.

ANDY. But at least we knew, Eugene, there'd now be a *third* trial. Times I had to cope, that's what held me. Knowin' that there'd be yet another day for the Scottsboro Boys! *(During Andy's speech, a fat old white woman — played by the actress depicting Victoria — has moseyed onto the stage. Her mask includes modern-day eyeglasses.)*

CHARLIE. And Mr. Leibowitz, he promise us that there come a time … *(Distracted.)* … that there come a time when … one day … the Scottsboro Boys … *(To the others, indicating the white woman.)* Isn't this supposed to come later? *(The Old White Woman continues to take in her surroundings, without ever reacting to any of the Scottsboro Boys.)*

HAYWOOD. *(Annoyed.)* Yeah, where the stage manager be?

ANDY. I know what this is. She tryin' to get her ass back in the story. You know how she always bitchin' 'bout bein' the forgotten victim in all this?

CLARENCE. Yeah, but no one gonna know who she is, when she all fat and old ugly!

HAYWOOD. Oh, somehow, I bet they do.

OLD VICTORIA. *(To the audience.)* In 1969, fella by the name of Dan T. Carter wrote himself a book. *Scottsboro,* he calls it, *A Tragedy of the American South.* On the very last page of his book, this man, Dan T. Carter, says that in 1961, Victoria Price died. *(A beat, then:)* Well I got news for y'all. I wuddn't dead. *(To the piano player.)* Go on, play monster music if you wanna! I don't give a shit. *(As the piano player complies … To the audience.)* I know what people think of me. All my life what they thought of me. Stuff that Judge Horton said when he's tossin' out the verdict. Which amounts to sayin' pretty much the same about every man on the jury! But don't you go on home just yet, all smug and satisfied. 'Cuz I guarantee you, *I will be back. (Lights fade.)*

End of Act One

ACT TWO

Scene 1

"A Medley"

HAYWOOD. Welcome back. Where've you been? Three years have passed! And even though the Attorney General is now the Lieutenant Governor, he's still handling the prosecution of the Scottsboro case since it was, after all, second only to the circus as the greatest show on earth. Ladies and gentlemen, let's meet the Lieutenant Governor of the State of Alabama … Thomas G. Knight, Jr. *(Piano fanfare as Knight enters.)*

KNIGHT. *(Sings, with piano.)*

ALL 'ROUND THE LITTLE FARM I WANDERED,
WHEN I WAS YOUNG;
THEN MANY HAPPY DAYS I SQUANDERED,
MANY THE SONGS I SUNG.

(Spoken.) Little something from Stephen Foster. Pretty, isn't it? We're blessed in this country with a collection of wonderful songs, which come from all our various cultures. For instance, there's that favorite Irish number … *(Piano intro, night club style.)*

KNIGHT.

OH DANNY BOY
THE PIPES, THE PIPES ARE CALLING,
FROM GLEN TO GLEN
AND DOWN THE MOUNTAIN SIDE

(Leibowitz strolls into the acting area, upstage of Knight.)

LEIBOWITZ and KNIGHT. *(Singing together.)*

THE SUMMER'S GONE AND ALL THE FLOWERS ARE DYING.

KNIGHT. Look who's here! Sam Liebowitz, ladies and gentlemen!

LEIBOWITZ. *(Sings.)*

'TIS YOU, 'TIS YOU MUST GO
AND I MUST ABIDE.

KNIGHT. All right! C'mon on over here, Sam! We were just reminiscin' in song about our diverse cultures. For instance, here's one of yours. *(Sings.)*

HA-VA NAGILA

HA-VA NAGILA

HA-VA NAGILA

VEH'NIS M'HUH!

(Privately to the audience, Leibowitz gives Knight's rendition a "so-so" gesture.) By the way, folks, that business about "Are we gonna let Alabama justice be bought and sold by Jew money from New York" … that *was* said, I admit, but I'd like to point out it was by *another* attorney. But, show biz bein' what it is, characters end up gettin' combined.

LEIBOWITZ. But on the other hand, that panty tossing?

KNIGHT. *(Can't help but grin:)* Yeah, okay. I did do that. *(Catching himself.)* But I apologized.

LEIBOWITZ. You know, Tom, I've been called a New York Jew, a Communist collaborator, a ruling class collaborator, and just about everything else during the course of this case … except what I am. *(The piano player leads in with an arpeggio.)* A courtroom lawyer. Someone committed to *one cause only:* my clients. Someone who will — and I make no apologies for this — use every trick in the book … to get these young men free! *(The piano player repeats the arpeggio. Leibowitz looks puzzled.)*

KNIGHT. Isn't there a song?

LEIBOWITZ. Huh?

KNIGHT. That's what we're doin' here, Sam. Reminiscin', singin' a few tunes …

BRODSKY. *(Enters, singing heartily.)*

ARISE, YOU PRISONERS OF STARVATION,

ARISE, YOU WRETCHED OF THE EARTH …

KNIGHT. Joe Brodsky, ladies and gentlemen!

BRODSKY.

FOR JUSTICE THUNDERS CONDEMNATION,

A BETTER WORLD'S IN BIRTH!

KNIGHT. Join us here, Joe, y'ol' rascal you! Tell me somethin'. How come you Communist bastards don't go live in Russia where you belong?

BRODSKY. Well, Tom, oddly enough, for de same reason as you. Y'see, I too am an American.

KNIGHT. Oh, so it's like … *(Sings, with piano.)*

THE UNION IS BEHIND US

WE SHALL NOT BE MOVED

(Knight continues in the background.)

BRODSKY. *(Over the singing, to the audience:)* And while dis may come as a surprise to some of yous, I love dis country, too. Because dis country hates injustice. But when a Communist sees injustice, radder den ask who … we ask *why.* De answer to which some folks find so upsettin' dat radder den face it, they would press for de death of dese boys again and again AND AGAIN *AND AGAIN!* *(Knight's singing has ended.)* Keep in mind, as I am *mocked* upon dis stage, dat had it not been for de Communists, dere wouldn't be any Scottsboro Boys. Dere would only be Nine More Dead Black Men. *(An uneasy moment. Then …)*

KNIGHT. Where's Walter? Christ, that man'll be late for his own funeral. *(Walter White enters, a bit sheepishly. The piano strikes up a fanfare.)* Walter White, ladies and gentlemen! *(Walter White rather reluctantly joins them, as the piano plays an upbeat, show biz version of "Swing Low Sweet Chariot.")* Well Walter, I'm sure I don't have to tell you that colored people have been second to none in their contribution to our rich heritage we're celebratin' here in song. Where to begin? What about … *(Sings and claps, with piano.)*

> I'M GONNA LAY DOWN MY SWORD AND SHIELD
> DOWN BY THE RIVERSIDE …

(Spoken.) Jump in anytime, Walt! *(Sings.)*

> DOWN BY THE RIVERSIDE …

(Spoken.) Or Sam? Joe?

KNIGHT, LEIBOWITZ and BRODSKY. *(Singing.)*

> DOWN BY THE RIVERSIDE.
> I'M GONNA LAY DOWN MY SWORD AND SHIELD …

(This continues in the background, eventually petering out, as …)

WALTER WHITE. *(To the audience, rather stiffly.)* Much has been made of the fact that the NAACP was not the first on the scene when this travesty of justice erupted. But I would like to ask: How were we to know these boys were innocent? For the Communists that was easy, since those lunatics will claim two and two are five if it serves their purpose.

KNIGHT. Uh, Walter, what we're doin' here is singin' songs? Maybe harmonizin'?

WALTER WHITE. One of these youngsters, don't forget, stated that a rape *did* take place! *(An aside to the audience.)* As a matter of fact, *three* of them did. But because it muddied up the drama, that little tidbit the playwright swept under the rug.

KNIGHT. *(Sings.)*

> HEY, HO, NOBODY HOME,
> MEAT NOR DRINK NOR MONEY HAVE I NONE

(The song is picked up as a round by Leibowitz and Brodsky, again eventually petering out, as …)

WALTER WHITE. *(Over the song.)* Maybe I am a stick in the mud. But I believe that, working within the system, American Negroes have made significant gains! Two Supreme Court decisions have resulted from this Scottsboro case alone! In

Powell vs. Alabama the court affirmed the right of every American, regardless of race, to adequate, competent, properly appointed defense counsel. And in *Norris vs. Alabama* the court declared that Negro citizens could no longer be excluded from juries! But you didn't see *that* depicted on this stage, did you? Because that, you see, isn't very theatrical! Yet it is in those dull, day-to-day details that the long, hard road to equality will be traversed! *(A moment, then …)*

KNIGHT. Thank you, Walter. Very rousing. Okay, time for a little white man's music! *(Sings, with piano.)*

>BEAUTIFUL DREAMER
>WAKE UNTO ME,
>STARLIGHT AND DEWDROPS
>ARE WAITING FOR THEE.

(Spoken.) Wherever I go, folks come up to me and ask why we pursued the prosecution of these boys trial after trial after trial.

LEIBOWITZ. Seems a fair question, given the absence of anything resembling evidence.

KNIGHT. Yeah, well, problem was, there came to be a good deal more to this case than evidence. For one thing, we had ol' Joe and his Commie pals holdin' rallies all over the world! Issuin' demands on Alabama! Now if we'd allowed that tactic to succeed, think what would be next. Plus, we had the likes of Sam here steppin' off the train. Now I take pride in Southern hospitality. But Sam's arrival was just a bit too reminiscent of the days of Reconstruction, when carpetbaggers came down here, claimin' to possess a superior morality, and tellin' us how to go about our affairs. Say, let's sing one of the great songs from Reconstruction! Gimme an intro, Skip. *(The piano player thinks, then shrugs.)* Guess there *aren't* any great songs from Reconstruction. Wonder why that is. Here's what it all boils down to. We've never come to grips with five words a few of our Foundin' Fathers sort of slipped in on us. "All men are created equal." I, for one, have never found where in the Bible the Creator says that — but be that as it may. If it *is* the case, then the colored race will build their community to a level equal to that of the whites. And if they are not equal, quite frankly, they will remain somethin' less. Or maybe become somethin' *more* I suppose I should add! Or maybe just become somethin' different. Which is all right. For that is our coat of many colors. Why did we persist in the prosecution of these boys? Not just to preserve southern culture, but *all* our cultures. Which is to say, America.

WALTER WHITE. *(Sings wistfully, crossing downstage.)*

>I HAD A DREAM THE OTHER NIGHT …

LEIBOWITZ. *(Crossing elsewhere.)*

>WHEN EVERYTHING WAS STILL …

KNIGHT. *(Crossing elsewhere.)*
    I DREAMED I SAW SUSANNA …
BRODSKY. *(Crossing elsewhere.)*
    SHE WAS WALKING 'CROSS THE HILL …
ALL FOUR. *(Slow and wistful, each in his own space.)*
    OH SUSANNA
    OH DON'T YOU CRY FOR ME.
    FOR I COME FROM ALABAMA
    WITH A BANJO ON MY KNEE.

Scene 2

Bare stage. The Scottsboro Boys languidly occupy the stage, much as they would their cells, after five years behind bars. Ozie speaks to the audience.

OZIE. One coconut, two nice cakes — chocolate and coconut — one pound mixed nuts, one dozen apples, one dozen oranges, one dozen bananas and candy.

CHARLIE. Ozie doin' his Christmas list to Mr. Brodsky.

OZIE. Three blocks of grape chewin' gum, two pairs of socks and some cheese and some fried rabbit and some sausage and some fried potato pies …

CHARLIE. Okay there, Ozie!

OZIE. … and some sauce meat and some Rexall toothpaste and some stamps and envelopes and paper.

HAYWOOD. What Ozie tryin' to say is we been in here now close to five years.

OZIE. *(Suddenly angry.)* WHY DON'T YOU ALL DO NOTHIN'?! *(No response. Nor even much in the way of reaction from any of the others.)* I wrote you and beg you like a dog to send me a guitar and you don't even answer my letter. But okay about that. Just take my next month eight dollar and get one.

HAYWOOD. Ozie talkin' here about the time while we's waitin' for our fourth trial.

ANDY. Wait a minute. What about the *third* trial?

HAYWOOD. I figure we can skip one.

OLEN. You can't just jump over it! Jesus, Haywood.

HAYWOOD. Look here, they ain't gonna follow all the legal shit. Hell, even *I* get confused!

OLEN. *(Stepping forward.)* Lemme have a crack at it.

HAYWOOD. Oh, man. *(To the audience, as he moves aside, irked.)* Any of y'all got pencil and paper may wanna take some notes.

OLEN. After Judge Horton threw out the second verdict, a new judge come on and they convicted us again. That was trial number three. *(To Haywood.)* Now how complicated was that?

HAYWOOD. Go on.

OLEN. Okay. So after that Mr. Leibowitz go on back up to the Supreme Court and got them to tell Alabama that they gotta try us a *fourth* time, on accounta there not bein' no black people on the jury rolls.

HAYWOOD. 'Cept there was some.

50

OLEN. Yeah, well … yeah. 'Cept then Mr. Leibowitz proved that those names got wrote in later. Which embarrassed the hell outa Alabama.

HAYWOOD. Right. They's so embarrassed, they kick our butts into solitary confinement!

OZIE. You can get some small six-string guitar and send it right away please. I need it.

HAYWOOD. Where we were left for over a year.

OZIE. Now you listen here! I ain't ask you for no eight-string guitar! I told you plain as I could speak to take my *eight dollar* and get me a *six*-string guitar! And I can't see why you ain't done sent it to me! You run a person crazy!

HAYWOOD. Ozie was havin' a lotta trouble holdin' up.

OZIE. Hope I didn't make you angry. Didn't mean any harm by it. Only tellin' you how I felt and what's more I could not help it. Seem like everybody mad at me.

CHARLIE. Ain't nobody mad at you personal, Ozie.

OZIE. *(Snarling at Charlie.)* That's enough of that! That'll do!

CHARLIE. Okay.

OZIE. This is a waste o' time! Let's move on!

HAYWOOD. *(To audience.)* He be talkin' about Judge Callahan now. The one who replace Judge Horton after he lose his election.

OLEN. That ol' cracker never even graduated college — let alone go to law school.

OZIE. I don't see the importance of that!

HAYWOOD. All these things Ozie sayin' is quotes.

OZIE. What is the use of that? You have gone over that!

OLEN. He was one son-of-a-bitch, tellin' everybody he gonna cut the Scottsboro case down to size.

OZIE. Nobody gonna touch my ding-dong! *(A beat. Then the others can't help but laugh.)*

HAYWOOD. *(To the audience, smiling.)* That ain't the judge he quotin' now. That be somethin' else.

OZIE. Nobody *ever* touch the ol' ding-dong.

WILLIE. Uh-oh. He gonna tell it now.

HAYWOOD. What Ozie sayin' here is there a certain place where you can always hide your dutch.

CHARLIE. Gotta tell 'em what you mean by dutch, Haywood.

HAYWOOD. A dutch can be *anythin'*, pretty much, that you work on 'til it get razor-sharp. Then you make a little slit and hide it in the zipper part of your pants. 'Cuz like Ozie say, even though they pat you down for weapons, no white man wanna touch a black man's privates. *(More snickers from the others.)*

51

ANDY. We all carried some kinda protection. Had to, you gonna survive where we was.

OZIE. *(Muttering.)* I'll kill the son-of-a-bitch. I'll kill the mother-fuckin' son-of-a-bitch.

HAYWOOD. *(To the other boys.)* Okay now, let's be clear to the people what went on. Since there been all kind of accusation.

OZIE. White mother-fuckin' bastard.

HAYWOOD. Charlie, how 'bout you be Sheriff Sandlin? Andy, you be Deputy Blalock. And Ozie, you and Clarence and Leroy be like you was, handcuffed together in the back seat of the car.

ANDY. I ain't doin' it with Ozie! Forget that, he's too crazy. Probably kill *me!*

OZIE. *(Still muttering.)* Seventy-fuckin'-five. Might as well be dead.

HAYWOOD. *(Responding to Andy.)* Okay, okay. Willie, how 'bout you be Ozie?

WILLIE. All right. *(The five appointed push together scenery, and then take seated positions, as if in a car. Meanwhile ...)*

HAYWOOD. *(To audience.)* What Ozie mean just now by seventy-five is that we be comin' back from bein' convicted for the fourth time. *(An aside.)* Actually it was just *my* fourth time. Olen simplified that.

OZIE. Oh boss, de boss couldn't do without me! Oh de boss, boss! Oh boss, de boss! Oh de boss, boss! Oh boss, de boss! ... *(Ozie continues this riff, fading it out as ...)*

HAYWOOD. I think what Ozie's referrin' to here is that, even though this time they had to call some black men to the jury selection, mostly the ones which showed found one excuse or another not to be sittin' on no jury. 'Specially ours.

CHARLIE. And what few brave ones was willin' they's able to dismiss.

HAYWOOD. So once again we watch as another bunch of white men end up sayin' ...

OZIE. *(Nasal white southern accent:)* We the jury find the defendant, Haywood Patterson, guilty as charged and fix the punishment at seventy-five years in the state penitentiary.

HAYWOOD. *(Taken aback.)* Well shut my mouth. There's progress. Leibowitz thought so, at least. For the first time in the history of Alabama, a black man convicted of rapin' a white woman wasn't given death. Just seventy-five years.

OLEN. Which I never understood. What was the point? That since they realize we innocent, we only get seventy-five years?

HAYWOOD. I think that about sums it up, yeah.

OLEN. I don't get that! If they know we innocent, why they keep convictin' us?!

CLARENCE. They hate blacks, Olen. Is that so hard to understand?

OLEN. For me it is.

HAYWOOD. Maybe Mr. Brodsky got it right. That they had to create hatred, to keep the system in place.

OLEN. Maybe. I don't know.

CHARLIE. Whatever it was, once again, we's handcuffed together and taken back to jail. Big police escort. Three to a car. Ozie and Clarence and Leroy be in the middle car.

OZIE. Be a lot better off get rid of that lawyer.

HAYWOOD. *(To audience.)* Afterward they say Ozie and Clarence and Leroy try to make an escape.

OZIE. Get yo'self a good, Christian Alabama man.

HAYWOOD. *(To audience.)* Now I want you to understand, this here's a two-door car. With two police officers, armed with pistols, sittin' in the front seat, which, if you in the back, gotta be push forward in order to get out.

OZIE. You niggers never gonna get out long as you got that New York Jewboy.

HAYWOOD. Got cops in the car behind. Cops in the car ahead. Not to mention National Guard. And them three handcuffed together tryin' to escape?

CLARENCE. Wasn't no escape that started it. Was Deputy Blalock, up front, makin' remarks about Mr. Leibowitz.

LEROY. 'Til Ozie finally fed up with it, make some remark back.

OZIE. You be quiet. *(In response to this, Andy, seated up front as if he were Deputy Blalock, turns and slaps Willie, depicting Ozie, across the face. For a moment, there is silence.)*

CLARENCE. Ozie, after that slap, didn't do nothin'. Didn't say nothin', either. No one did. We just drives another couple miles, each keepin' our own thoughts, until — *(Clarence is interrupted by Willie grabbing Andy by the head and slashing his neck.)*

OZIE. MOTHER FUCKER! MOTHER FUCKER! ... *(Andy hollers as Ozie's rant continues. Leroy and Clarence scream.)*

CHARLIE. *(Depicting Sheriff Sandlin.)* Hey! Hey!

EUGENE. All we know in the third car is that the car up ahead suddenly be swervin' this way and that! *(Charlie gets up and runs around to where Willie, seated by the window, is now struggling with Andy, still hollering as Willie is now trying to grab his gun. Throughout, Ozie is continuing to shout "Mother Fucker!" over and over as ...)*

OLEN. Then when it skid to a stop, the sheriff jump out, drawin' his gun, and run over and open the car door and ...

CHARLIE. BAM! *(Ozie's shouts suddenly stop. A pause.)*

CLARENCE. Leroy and me, we right away holds up our hands — which also lift up Ozie's floppy hand — and we say ...

CLARENCE   LEROY
Ain't us, boss! We ain't   We didn't do it! We don't done nothin', boss!
got no part of this!

CLARENCE. And by then, the other cars has pulled to a stop, and they all around us with their guns and rifles ready.

LEROY. And Ozie's just slumped over dead.

CLARENCE. And the deputy he slashed is staggerin' outa the car now, clutchin' at his neck.

LEROY. Blood seepin' out past his hands. And blood splattered on the windshield. And all over the car. All over us.

CLARENCE. One of the police start to uncuff Ozie from me and another yell, "You leave them niggers like they are! Drive 'em on over to the nearest jail and this time leave the door open!" And another of 'em say, "Naw, we can't do that. We gotta get this nigger to a hospital." And another of 'em say, "Don't look like there no need for that."

HAYWOOD. Deputy Blalock they rush to the hospital in the nearby town of Cullman, Alabama. Where they stitch him up and he be home that night.

OZIE. I ain't never been shot before.

CLARENCE. Holy Jesus!

LEROY. I admit, I about peed in my pants when he said that!

HAYWOOD. Turned out, ol' Ozie wasn't dead! So they drove him to Hillman Hospital, where they treat the colored ... (Turning to the others.) ... which was how far, would you say?

CLARENCE. Forty miles. And they take their time, too.

HAYWOOD. Doctors there found the bullet one inch inside Ozie's brain. Give him a fifty-fifty chance. But damn if ol' Ozie didn't live!

OLEN. Ain't ever been the same though.

HAYWOOD. Yeah, well ... who of us is, Olen? (Olen, finding he has no answer, turns away; goes off to his personal space.)

CHARLIE. Ozie's mama come to see him in the hospital.

ANDY. But the police only let her in after she show a furniture receipt, with her name on it, to prove she was his mama.

CHARLIE. And o' course they in there listenin' to everythin' she say. "Here your mama, boy. She come to see you."

CLARENCE. Ozie lyin' there all doped up.

CHARLIE. "Ozie," she say, "do you hurt?"

OZIE. Not now.

CHARLIE. "What you do that for, child? Why you cut that man?"

OZIE. I done give up, mama. Everybody mad at me.

ANDY. Nobody mad at you personal, Ozie.

HAYWOOD. And then come the last thing he say to her. Tell 'em, Ozie.

OZIE. Don't let Sam Leibowitz have nothin' more to do with my case.

Scene 3

Bare stage. Ozie, who now has a guitar, tries to pick out "Oh Susanna." Clarence sweeps his area. Two others confer over something private. Willie approaches Olen with a piece of paper.

WILLIE. Will you read my letter to Miss Damon?

OLEN. *(Indicating audience.)* No, Willie, you're supposed to read it to *them*, remember?

HAYWOOD. *(To audience.)* Bear with us on this. We hopin' to try a little somethin' different. Lettin' the younger ones, who be the quietest, tell their piece of it.

CHARLIE. *(To audience.)* Willie wanted to read his letter to Miss Damon. Who the lady that replace Mr. Brodsky, when they, I don't know, get rid of him or whatever.

HAYWOOD. They didn't get rid of him! He just kinda move to the background.

OLEN. Or lose interest, more like it.

HAYWOOD. He didn't lose no damn interest, Olen!

CHARLIE. You gotta figure, what with *six* years now this thing be draggin' on, them Reds had better things to do.

HAYWOOD. Didn't see so much of Mr. Liebowitz, either, I might point out.

CHARLIE. Yeah, that true, too. He also step outa the spotlight, on accounta bein' the cause of so much animosity.

OLEN. And an accounta bein' busy again defendin' murderers with money and other high society types.

ANDY. *(Joining them.)* And anyway there was a new guy now, who come to see us one day, by the name of Mr. Chalmers. Told us he the head of the Scottsboro Defense Committee.

HAYWOOD. Whoever they were.

OLEN. I think the point is who they were *not*. Not Communists. Not northerners. Not Jews.

LEROY. So is Willie gonna get to read his letter? *(A beat, then ...)*

HAYWOOD. Oh. Right. Go ahead, Willie. Nice and loud.

WILLIE. Remember the new guy come to see me?

HAYWOOD. What new guy come to see you?

CLARENCE. *(Joining them.)* Yeah, when was that? What he want?

WILLIE. You don't remember? That one day that man come to see me? And say to me, "Willie, I know we never been introduced, but I am your father." *(A moment.)*

HAYWOOD. *(Softly.)* I do remember that day, Willie, now that you mention it.

CHARLIE. *(To audience.)* Willie's mama pass when he be but a baby.

HAYWOOD. Fact is, we about the only family Willie ever know.

WILLIE. That hadn't kicked me out like my aunt, or get old and die like gramma. My daddy I never even knew who he was!

HAYWOOD. Until you become a Scottsboro Boy, that is.

CLARENCE. Old bastard probably figured he get himself a piece of something.

ANDY. Point is, we saw all kinda faces come and go. Even the prosecutor — who get elected lieutenant governor but still keep on the case! — even he, one day, up and died. Six years in, seem like all the faces had changed.

LEROY. 'Cept ours.

CLARENCE. Got that right.

ANDY. No, actually, yours too, little brother! And Eugene's! The two of you sproutin' mustaches. Turnin' into men!

OLEN. That be the thing in prison. Some of life stops and some of life don't. Make it hard to keep your footin'. *(Clarence, Charlie and Andy concur.)*

HAYWOOD. Okay, Willie, I think that sets things up. Go ahead and read your letter. Nice and loud.

WILLIE. *(Steps forward, reads.)* Dear Miss Damon …

EUGENE. You so full of shit, Haywood.

HAYWOOD. *(A moment, then:)* Say what?

EUGENE. You heard me. You are so full of shit. What're you, the daddy here? *(From the others, quietly: "Uh-oh," etc.)*

HAYWOOD. You got somethin' on your mind, Eugene?

EUGENE. What I got on my mind ain't none of your damn business. And it certainly ain't none of *theirs! (Meaning us.)*

HAYWOOD. Well now, if you don't want to participate in this, Eugene, I don't see anyone sayin' you have to.

EUGENE. 'Cept the State of Alabama. *(The others snort and chuckle. "He right about that," "Got you there, Haywood," etc.)*

HAYWOOD. *(Holds a moment, then to the audience:)* See, folks, like any family, we have our ups and downs. Gettin' along some days, and some days not. And — probably like your family, too — there always be one, usually in their teens, wishin' they wasn't related.

EUGENE. Where you gettin' this family shit? I got a family.

HAYWOOD. We a family, Eugene. Whether you like it or not.

EUGENE. You wish. Don't forget, I knew you in Chattanooga. *(To audience.)* Haywood just wantin' us to be a family on accounta he afraid of bein' free. 'Cuz then what he do? Then who he be? Just another nigger. And not a very talented one at that! Bein' a Scottsboro Boy the best thing that ever happen to Haywood! Like gettin' selected into some club! Walkin' and talkin' with the whites ...

ANDY. Okay, Eugene. You made the point.

CLARENCE. He gonna get you later, you don't hush. *(Haywood, through this, has said nothing. He is poker-faced.)*

EUGENE. *(Glances at Haywood, then to audience, defiantly.)* Bein' a Scottsboro Boy the best thing that ever happen to Haywood. But not me. *(Eugene goes off to his personal space. After a moment ...)*

ANDY. Okay, Willie, go ahead.

WILLIE. *(Reading.)* Dear Miss Damon. Thank you for tellin' me all about the rain you be gettin' in New York. I would be grateful to hear also somethin' about our case.

LEROY. Fat chance of that. They don't ever write us nothin' 'bout the case!

CLARENCE. Yeah, but you know why that is.

LEROY. On accounta the warden read every letter that come to us, I know. But still, month after month we wait for someone to come see us, and even then don't get the answers to our questions! Things like: How this ever gonna end? How you gonna get us outa here? 'Cuz I'm gettin' to be a grown man now! — I got a girlfriend back home! — or *had* one, anyway. For all I know, she off and married now. Since she don't read or write, and my mama don't say, I don't rightly know, but I kinda expect she off and fuckin' someone else.

ANDY. Leroy.

LEROY. Truth be told, I kinda think she was hikin' up her skirt for other men even before I get into this mess.

ANDY. We were hopin' you would talk about the case.

LEROY. I *am* talkin' 'bout the case! You leave me be! *(To audience.)* See, what I don't understand is why, back when I be but thirteen — *twelve*, in fact, the first time! — she be so willin'. That somethin' I never understood — and still don't — except to say that, before this shit, I didn't know nothin'. I was so trustin'. Life was so fine. And now, lookin' back on those days, I find myself thinkin': What a sick bitch she musta been. Or else just stupid. 'Cuz what was in it for her? 'Cuz now I know somethin' always in it for someone, 'less they gettin' robbed or raped. *(A moment or two, then:)* Most days, that's what I think about. Her. Most days I can't get my mind on nothin' else. What she was like. What she like now? What was in it for her? Thinkin' over every inch of her! Thinkin' how I just got to get out of here. *I got to get out!* *(A moment, then:)* Otherwise, I be better off dead. *(Andy comes up and puts an arm around Leroy.)*

ANDY. *(To audience.)* Fact is, freedom was somethin' we was all startin' to smell. Somethin' that, when all this first happen, I don't think even crossed our minds. Back then it was survivin'. But now, it was bein' free.

HAYWOOD. And not just any ol' free, either. Tell 'em, Andy.

ANDY. Even though the lawyers don't say nothin' — on accounta not puttin' anythin' important in our mail — we started gettin' a sense that somethin' was in the works. Certain snide remarks from the guards maybe it was. Or the tone in the letters from Miss Damon. Or maybe that Mr. Liebowitz, who was always full of fight, wasn't like that anymore. Things like that got us optimistic.

OLEN. In prison, you learn a lot from what's not spoken.

CLARENCE. One day, this Mr. Chalmers, the new guy from the new group, put it to us. What would we think about pleadin' guilty, with the assurance that the sentence would be seven years? With time served, we'd be out before too long!

CHARLIE. Andy was the first to answer. Didn't even think about it, either. Didn't consult with us or nothin'! Just said no.

ANDY. Damn right I did. I'd rot there till I die, rather than say I did what I did *not.*

HAYWOOD. Any one of us coulda took that deal. Got our ass out. Raised questions 'bout the innocence of the others. But not one did. Not one. Not one. *(A moment, then:)* Maybe we be a family, after all. *(They retire to their private places. Except for Willie, still holding his letter.)*

WILLIE. *(After a moment or two, reads:)* I am nineteen years old. I have brown skin and brown eyes and black hair. I like dancin', motion pictures, parties, swimmin', the guitar, and tennis. Could you please send me a picture?

Scene 4

"Big Deal"

SCOTTSBORO BOY. *(As an aside.)* Any of you takin' notes may want to get them pencils ready again. *(Announces.)* After the *fourth* conviction of Haywood Patterson, the state still had to go through the motions of trying Clarence Norris for the *third* time, and all us others for the *second* time. So in July, 1937, Sam Leibowitz returned to Alabama to do battle once again. Ladies and gentlemen, here now are Thomas Knight and Samuel Leibowitz, presenting their fancy footwork ... leading up to the final trial. *(Lively piano introduction as Leibowitz and Knight come dancing out, with straw hats and canes.)*

LEIBOWITZ. *(Sings.)*

    OH, TOMMY,

    I HEAR YOU'RE IN NEW YORK.

    THEY SAY YOU'RE STAYING AT THE WALDORF,

    AND GOT A BOTTLE TO UNCORK.

    OH OH OH, TOMMY!

    I CAN'T BE SEEN THERE.

    WHY NOT SLIP UP TO MY APARTMENT?

    HAVE A LITTLE DINNER.

(They dance. Tap dance would be wonderful but soft shoe will suffice. They punctuate their steps with alternate shouts of "Okay!" ... "All right!" ... "I'll take the A-train!" ... "Watch your wallet!" then ...)

KNIGHT. *(Sings.)*

    OH, SAMMY!

    I HEAR FROM GOVERNOR GRAVES

    THIS SCOTTSBORO CASE

    IS EGG ON ALABAMMY'S FACE.

LEIBOWITZ.

    DON'T I KNOW IT, TOMMY!

    I KNOW HOW YOU FEEL.

    I'M OUTA GROUNDS FOR APPEAL.

    LET'S MAKE A DEAL!

KNIGHT.

    OH YEAH-YEAH, SAMMY!

WHY DON'T WE CHANGE THE ACCUSATION
TO HANKY-PANKY AND FLIRTATION
THEY'LL DO A LITTLE TIME FOR MISCEGENATION.

LEIBOWITZ. Whoa! Tommy! *(Leibowitz does a solo dance turn. Knight, looking on, snaps his fingers in rhythm. Leibowitz punctuates his moves this time with intermittent shouts of "No way!" … "No sir!" … "No how!" and finally, "Try this one!" before returning to …)*

SUPPOSE, MISTER TOMMY,
Y'ALL LET THE YOUNGEST ONES WALK
AND THE OTHER FIVE SAY SIMPLE ASSAULT
WOULD YOU BE APPALLED?

KNIGHT.

OY GEVALT, SAMMY!
I LOVE THE WAY YOU SAY "Y'ALL."

LEIBOWITZ.

THEN TELL ME WHY, TOMMY!
YOU'VE STOPPED RETURNING MY CALLS.

(The two of them now dance a soft shoe. Sometimes together, sometimes not, calling out things like, "Thought we had a deal there!" … "Gotta watch my step!" … "Why what's the problem?" Suddenly, Knight staggers for a few steps, then collapses. Leibowitz, wondering if he's clowning or not, dances on another moment or two, then stops. The piano too peters out. Knight lies in a heap, perfectly still. Leibowitz kneels down next to him. The other Scottsboro Boys apprehensively draw near.)

LEIBOWITZ. *(Quietly.)* Oh my God.

A SCOTTSBORO BOY. What's happened?

ANOTHER SCOTTSBORO BOY. He have a heart attack?

LEIBOWITZ. *(Nods, then:)* He's dead, fellas. *(Leibowitz stands. The piano plays an introductory series of melancholy chords as Leibowitz crosses downstage to sing. As he opens his mouth …)*

KNIGHT. *(Leaping back to life.)*

OH, SAMMY!!!
WHY THE LONG FACE?
DON'T BE SO NAMBY-PAMBY!
SOMEONE ELSE'LL TAKE MY PLACE!

LEIBOWITZ. *(Calls out.)* Okay, everybody up! Final trial! *(Leibowitz and Knight fling their arms over each other's shoulder — thus forming a two man kickline. They thus kick various of the Scottsboro Boys as …)*

KNIGHT. Guilty! … Guilty! … You too! … And both o' you! *(Knight and Leibowitz separate back into a soft shoe step. As they do …)* Take it, Sammy!

(Knight gets Leibowitz's cane and tosses it to him. The dancing Leibowitz uses his cane either to point to or pull various of the Scottsboro Boys to him, as …)
LEIBOWITZ. Not guilty! … Acquitted! … Take a walk, son! … You're free!
LEIBOWITZ and KNIGHT.
(Dancing and singing together.)

>OH ALABAMA!
>SAY G'BYE TO ALL THE DRAMA!
>WE'D LIKE TO EXPLAIN, UHHH …
>BUT WE GOT TO CATCH A TRAIN!

(Waving as they shuffle off in opposite directions.)

>OH, ALL OF YOU OTHER BOYS!
>RIGHT NOW WE'RE JUST OVERJOYED!
>WE'LL SEND YOU A POSTCARD FROM
>MANHATTAAAAN!

Scene 5

Bare stage. Haywood speaks to the audience. The others remain quietly at the periphery.

HAYWOOD. Andy and Clarence wrote letters that night. To the people in New York. I didn't have no words to say. I don't think I ever felt so low in all my life. I be happy for Leroy and Eugene. And Willie and Olen. But how come they didn't choose me? Sometime it seem like half my life been spent wonderin', "Why not me?" And the other half wonderin', "Why me?" I don't care what no one says, we was done dirty. For a while we'd been hearin' talk of a deal. And Andy over there made it clear as day, that time when they ask if we agree to some kinda guilty plea, *ain't no way!* And now Leibowitz tellin' us he don't know what happened that afternoon? That Alabama just dumped 'em? I believe *everybody* lyin' to us now. They say to us, don't you worry, the governor gonna take care of this. 'Cuz he agree it make no sense that four be let go while we be kept on the same evidence! Well when he gonna let us go, we ask. Well, he be leavin' office come a year from December. A year from December! That be another *year and a half!* Leibowitz and the others they say, y'all got to be patient. Down where I was, which now was at Atmore State Prison, they run a farm gots lots of snakes. Black snakes mostly, can't hurt you none. Still there's somethin' about snakes give people the creeps. I think it be that … *snakes is patient.* So the next time I come up on one, I find myself lookin' him in the eye — and he at me — and thinkin' to him, "We know each other now, don't we?" I pick up that snake, and slung him 'round my neck and left him there the rest of the day. I got to wearin' lots of 'em like that, like they be my jewelry. Snake Eye, the other prisoners take to callin' me, on accounta my own face gettin' that look. Steady and patient.

CHARLIE. Come to the point, Haywood.

HAYWOOD. *(No hurry.)* Year-and-a-half go by, and come a day they take me to Birmingham. To the governor's office. Handcuffed. I get in there, Governor Graves sittin' behind his desk, he get up and say to me, "Haywood, Clarence tells me he like to kill you. What you got to say about that?" "Nothin'," I tell him. "Well why do you suppose he say a thing like that?" And I say, "I don't know nothin' about what Clarence say."

CLARENCE. Oh fuck you don't!

HAYWOOD. *(Wheeling around to Clarence.)* You watch your filthy ass, man!

63

(They go for each other, as …)
CLARENCE. I'll cut your fuckin' dick off, you ever touch my girl [again!] —
HAYWOOD. *(Overlapping.)* He ain't your girl! *I* BOUGHT HIM! *(All the other Scottsboro Boys intervene to keep Haywood and Clarence from killing each other, as …)*
CLARENCE. The fuck you did!
HAYWOOD. I PAID MY MONEY!
CLARENCE. THAT OL' WOLF OWE ME TWICE THAT MONEY! HE GOT NO BUSINESS SELLIN' THAT BOY TO YOU! — *SHE IS MINE! (A pause. It is Haywood, finally, who steps away from this, returning to the audience.)*
HAYWOOD. *(Shaken, ashamed.)* Well … the beans is spilled now, I guess. Needless to say, so much for the pardon. *(Takes a moment to collect himself, but, upset, he's isn't getting collected.)* How 'bout it, Eugene? Maybe sing one o' your faggot songs, why don't ya? Oughta be real touchin'. *(No answer. Eugene turns away. Pulling himself together to some degree.)* After that episode, Alabama say the case is closed. They say from here on out … *(Finding his voice wavering here:)* … there be no more Scottsboro Boys. *(A breath.)* We handle their cases one at a time. Five years later, they let Charlie out real quiet. And a little after that, I shakes hands with my old friend Andy, and shake Clarence's hand, too. Even Ozie, despite stabbin' the sheriff, go free in, I dunno, 1946 or somethin'. Only one left after that is me. Way I see it, everyone I ever known has let me down. Or else, like my mama, has died and gone. Leibowitz and all them do-gooders let me down. God knows the governor let me down. And God Himself, I some-times feel, let me down, too. Only one left to depend on now is me. So I fixes on a plan. They got me sweepin' floors inside the prison. But where I needs be is out on the farm. So I get myself in a little trouble and they bring me to the war-den for a whippin'. And I make just like Brer Rabbit. "Oh don't send me to the farm, cap'n! Whip me if you gotta but please don't be sendin' me to the farm!" Which o' course they do. But I'm assigned to Shotgun Smith, and ain't nobody ever escaped from him. Though there be several that died tryin'. All I can do is … be patient. Then in the winter of '48, he retire. And they put a rookie in his place. But still I bide my time. 'Til well into summer, when the leaves be full and the corn be high. And I invited several others to go with me, pointin' out how good their chances is, on accounta the guards first be sendin' the hounds after me. But really what I be usin' 'em for was bait. Come mid-July, I decide the time has come to grant myself a pardon. So as the sun be startin' to set one day, I give the nod, and we scatter through the corn! One young kid I kept with me, case I needed a sacrifice. The others head out as fast and far as possible, the fools. Me and the boy, we stay close, listenin' to the dogs gradually roundin' all them oth-

ers up. After dark, me and the boy ease into the woods. But then he start talkin' about stealin' a car to get away. I tell him forget that. But them dogs barkin' is makin' him scared. Across the road there be a farm and he decide to make a dash for their garage. No sooner he start off runnin' than there's shouts and shots. Shit, I'm thinkin', that gonna draw the dogs for sure! I don't know what become of that boy, but me I double back to where there be a stream about waist-high. Figure maybe the water hide my scent. But damn if them dogs ain't comin' closer. And through the trees, I see the headlights pullin' up on the road. A whole posse of 'em. The dogs I can tell is comin' though the corn field. Next they be here in the woods. Ain't nothin' for it now, Haywood — 'lessn you can make yourself into a snake. Them dogs already splashin' in the water. I can see 'em. Two that's jumped on in and one be waitin' at the edge, woofin' and wailin'. Good boy. You a good boy. That lead dog he look at me sorta funny, still goin' arf! arf! arf! Come here, boy. People be treatin' you like a dog all your life, c'mere to me. Come on. And the second dog too now start watchin' kinda close. Yeah, you a good boy. C'mere to Haywood. And that front dog kind of nuzzle on up to me, and I take his head in my hands and thrust it under the water. And to the second one I be sayin', "Oh, he's a good dog. And you a good dog too, you know that?" And underwater I feel that hound kickin' and strugglin'. "C'mon to me, boy," I say to that second dog, who be lookin' at me kinda queer now. "Come on over here to Haywood." And the first dog, he finally beginnin' to slow down under the water there. And when he stop, I reach out to the second one and say, "It's okay. Come to Haywood." And I kill him too, same as the first. And that dog over by the edge, he ain't sayin' nothin'. He don't seem to know what all's goin' on. C'mere, boy. You a good dog, too. But I don't guess he believed that, since he just turned and hunkered off. All the next day I stay on the prison grounds, knowin' it be the last place they look. And then I set out, travelling at night through the stream … like a snake.

Scene 6

"The Fat Lady Sings"

The piano plays a few introductory bars of "While Choo-Chooin' to Chattanooga" as ... Old Victoria, the fat rural white woman in eyeglasses who earlier promised to return, pads onto the stage. This time she's dressed for court, carrying a little purse, wearing a hat and a pin.

OLD VICTORIA. *(To audience.)* Where were you on the night of Thursday, April 22, 1976? *(Waits, then:)* You don't know? Well hell, *you* wouldn't do too good under cross-examination then either, would ya? So happens, I can tell you the whereabouts of forty-one *million* people that particular night. They was in front of their TV sets watching two hours of sex and violence parading around under the title of *Judge Horton and the Scottsboro Boys.*

HAYWOOD. Oh, man. *(To the others.)* I have never understood the point of doin' this part.

OLD VICTORIA. *(Still to the audience, unfazed.)* Once again, my privacy was violated.

ANDY. It's all part of the show, Haywood.

OLD VICTORIA. My good name defamed. Once again — only this time it was on NBC — I got raped.

HAYWOOD. Oh, why don't you go fuck yourself?

EUGENE. Haywood!

HAYWOOD. 'Bout the only way the fat ol' bitch gonna get anything.

EUGENE. Hey, c'mon, let her do her act.

HAYWOOD. Her act?

OLD VICTORIA. *(Unflustered and undaunted.)* Once again, forty-five years after the fact, I found myself in a court of law, seeking justice.

OLEN. Not to mention five or six million dollars.

HAYWOOD. Got that right!

EUGENE. Hey, hush, both you.

OLD VICTORIA. It was like a nightmare revisited.

HAYWOOD. *(His anger getting the better of him now.)* Dammit, bitch, *you* the fuckin' nightmare!

OLD VICTORIA. "How many of them boys penetrated your private parts, Ms.

66

Price?" they ask me all over again. "Were you bleedin' from your private parts?" "Ms. Price, could you please describe to the court your private parts?"

HAYWOOD. Hows about you just climb up your private parts and disappear! *(Some of the boys hoot at this; others, though amused, admonish Haywood. Old Victoria doesn't react.)*

OLD VICTORIA. It was like it was the 1930s all over.

CLARENCE. 'Cept for the fact that this time, you didn't get the verdict you wanted, did you?

OLD VICTORIA. *(To audience.)* I told the truth.

HAYWOOD. Answer the man's question. They kicked your fat ass outa that court house, didn't they?

OLD VICTORIA. *(To audience.)* I told it in every trial.

HAYWOOD. HEY! DIDN'T YOU HEAR HIM ASKIN' YOU SOMETHIN'?!

CHARLIE. Leave her be, Haywood. She just an old lady now.

HAYWOOD. SHE AN OLD *WITCH* IS WHAT SHE IS! *(Pulls out a "dutch" hidden in the seam of the fly of his pants.)* I say let's kill her!

ANDY. Haywood! Put down the dutch!

EUGENE. Hey, that ain't the way the show ends!

HAYWOOD. Well, what do you say we *change* the way it ends?

OLD VICTORIA. *(To the audience, unfazed.)* There has been over a thousand pages.

CHARLIE. The show's why we here, Haywood!

OLD VICTORIA. And every one of my pages is alike.

OLEN. Change the ending … and it'd be the end of us.

OLD VICTORIA. And if I had to do it all over, it would be the same thing again. *(A moment, then:)*

HAYWOOD. Well, I'd do it *different!* *(Haywood lunges at her, weapon raised.)*

ANDY. HAYWOOD! *(Old Victoria continues not to react as … It takes Andy, Charlie and Clarence to restrain Haywood.)*

HAYWOOD. *(Struggling furiously to break loose.)* I'M ENDIN' THIS SHOW! I'M ENDIN' THIS SHOW!

CHARLIE. *(Overlapping Haywood.)* Don't you be doin' something you gonna be sorry for!

HAYWOOD. SHE CAN'T HURT ME! AIN'T NOTHIN' SHE CAN DO TO ME AIN'T ALREADY BEEN DONE!

ANDY. Leave her be, Haywood! It's over. Let it alone now.

HAYWOOD. It *ain't* over!

ANDY. Haywood, it's done! She dead now. We all of us are.

HAYWOOD. But she ain't dead, Andy! She wasn't when they put that show on the TV, and I swear she ain't now! I know she ain't!

ANDY. She died, Haywood. Five years after that lawsuit of hers. She finally gone. *(A beat, then:)*

LEROY. *We* ain't dead. Are we?

HAYWOOD. Yeah, what you be tellin' him that for?

LEROY. *(Approaching his brother.)* Are we, Andy?

ANDY. *(After some consideration.)* I don't know exactly, little brother.

HAYWOOD. The Scottsboro Boys will never die.

OLEN. Then there ain't no point in killing her then, is there? Seeing as she still won't die. Be best just let her tell the folks what she come to say and get on with it. *(Haywood's rage is spent. He is released.)*

OLD VICTORIA. *(To audience.)* Truth will stand where a lie will fall. *(Old Victoria holds a moment, then turns and starts to exit. But her way is blocked by some of the Scottsboro Boys. She stops and turns to go the other way. That way, too, is now blocked by Scottsboro Boys. For the first time in the play, she looks at them, and they at her. Startled.)* What is this? W-What do you all want? My purse? Is that it? *(Extending it, frightened.)* Here, g-go 'head! Have it! *(The Scottsboro Boys look at each other, themselves taken aback.)* Have my w-wrist watch too if you want it! And m-my p-pin! Here. I don't need 'em! *(She has removed these items too and, cowering, has extended them to her would-be muggers.)*

HAYWOOD. *(His contempt palpable.)* Hello, Victoria. *(A pause. Victoria eyes him, then the others, then says …)*

OLD VICTORIA. I beg your pardon, do I know you? *(Haywood doesn't answer.)*

CHARLIE. Fact is, Haywood, she *never* knew we existed. *(Old Victoria, baffled by this whole encounter, apprehensively turns, and plods away.)*

Scene 7

Bare stage.

LEROY. She gone now?

EUGENE. *(Who has watched her go off.)* I hope so. *(Haywood remains still, his encounter with Old Victoria continuing to haunt him. The others are aware of this, as they gather up their belongings and put them back in the trunks and crates.)*

ANDY. Shit, she find out about this play, she sue *our* ass for sure, huh Haywood? *(Haywood doesn't respond.)*

OLEN. Tell ya this. I wouldn't mind suin' some butt. *(To audience.)* That vaude-ville show we was in wasn't nothin' like this here!

EUGENE.	LEROY.
Yeah. Tell 'em what we really did.	That's right. Wasn't much of anything.

OLEN. All we did was act out a scene from our trial, and then they had the four of us sing a song. Kinda like you talked about, Haywood? With singing and sol-idarity and such? *(No response, or very little.)* Anyway, only did it a week.

LEROY. But it beat Leibowitz and the NAACP, tryin' to keep us separated! Spread around in jobs they found for us, or vocational schools for some. Anythin' but in the news.

EUGENE. Or home. *(Leroy, Olen and Willie acknowledge that.)* Anyplace but home, they say. On accounta the trouble it might cause. *(A moment, then:)*

WILLIE. I got a job.

OLEN. Yeah, you did, Willie. You did okay. And Charlie, too, later on, down in Atlanta, married and all. And you, too, Clarence — you did okay.

CLARENCE. *(Waves this away.)* Too many wives. And the gamblin' bug got me. But what about you, Olen? Bumming money whenever you passin' through New York. You turned into a drinkin' man.

OLEN. If it ain't one thing it be another.

CLARENCE. And Andy I stopped hearing ever since ... that business with your brother.

ANDY. You gonna tell about that, Leroy?

LEROY. I don't have nothin' to say about it.

ANDY. *(To audience.)* My little brother come home one time from the mer-chant marine to find his wife had taken up with another man. Leroy got so mad, he shot her. Killed her. Then, huggin' a Bible to his side, he killed himself.

CHARLIE. Tell about you, Haywood.

HAYWOOD. Naw. Show's over. *(The others chime in, "Ain't over yet," "No, it isn't," "C'mon now." To audience.)* I went on to live underground. Havin' escaped. Bein' helped in my hidin' by people in the Civil Rights Congress, which is what the International Labor Defense joined into once it close up shop. One of the people who help me be a man name of Earl Conrad. Me and him wrote a book we call *Scottsboro Boy*. Two weeks after it get published, the FBI arrest me in Detroit. But the governor of Michigan refuse to send me back to Alabama. And so I was free.

ANDY. For about six month.

HAYWOOD. Yeah, well, that another matter.

OLEN. All part of the show, Haywood. *(As Haywood speaks, the others begin to gather together upstage, as if preparing to leave once he's finished.)*

HAYWOOD. Up there in Detroit one night, I go into a bar. Had a bunch of copies of my book I be tryin' to sell. And there be some remarks made and a fight — and not just me in it, either — and when it over, this one fella be dead. Which, way I look at it, was self-defense! Anyway no matter. Right after I'm convicted, they find some kinda cancer. And that be that.

CLARENCE. Ain't you gonna tell 'em about my book?

HAYWOOD. Oh yeah, Clarence here wrote a book, too. With the help of some woman. Not as good as mine though.

CLARENCE. Up yours, Haywood!

HAYWOOD. *(Happy to have gotten his goat.)* Called his *The Last of the Scottsboro Boys*. Which I guess maybe he be … *(Turning to the others.)* … unless any o' you others care to step back into the public view? *(No takers. To audience.)* So I guess maybe Clarence be the last, who knows? *(A moment.)* I guess maybe the show be over now.

ANDY. Ain't ever over, Haywood. *(Haywood hears this, then, defiant to the last, turns to the audience and says …)*

HAYWOOD. Who knows, Andy? *(Haywood dons his cap as the piano commences to reprise "Manchild Don't You Cry." He rejoins the other Scottsboro Boys, again as they were at the outset of the play. To the audience.)* Who knows? *(As the lights fade to black, Haywood gives the audience a farewell wave.)*

End of Play

LYRICS

Verse from "We Shall Not be Moved" *[Traditional]*

THE UNION IS BEHIND US
WE SHALL NOT BE MOVED
THE UNION IS BEHIND US
WE SHALL NOT BE MOVED
JUST LIKE A TREE THAT'S STANDING BY THE WATER
WE SHALL NOT BE MOVED.

Verse from "Hey, Ho, Nobody Home" *[Traditional]*

HEY, HO, NOBODY HOME,
MEAT NOR DRINK NOR MONEY HAVE I NONE
YET I WILL BE MER-R-R-R-R-Y
HEY, HO, NOBODY HOME.

Verse from "Study War No More" *[Traditional]*

I'M GONNA LAY DOWN MY SWORD AND SHIELD,
DOWN BY THE RIVERSIDE,
DOWN BY THE RIVERSIDE,
DOWN BY THE RIVERSIDE,
I'M GONNA LAY DOWN MY SWORD AND SHIELD,
DOWN BY THE RIVERSIDE,
STUDY WAR NO MORE.

(Chorus)

I AIN'T GONNA STUDY WAR NO MORE,
I AIN'T GONNA STUDY WAR NO MORE,
I AIN'T GONNA STUDY WAR NO MORE,
I AIN'T GONNA STUDY WAR NO MORE,
I AIN'T GONNA STUDY WAR NO MORE,
I AIN'T GONNA STUDY WAR NO MORE.

SONG CREDITS AND NOTES

"Manchild Don't You Cry," music and lyrics by Harley White, Jr.

"Choo-chooing to Chattanooga," music by Harley White, Jr., words by Mark Stein

"Ruby," music and lyrics by Harley White, Jr.

"My Old Kentucky Home," by Stephen Foster (1853)

"Danny Boy," traditional

"Hava-Na Gila", traditional

"The Internationale," by Eugene Potter & Pierre Degeyter (1888)

"We Shall Not Be Moved," traditional

"Down by the Riverside," traditional

"Hey-Ho, Nobody Home," traditional

"Beautiful Dreamer," by Stephen Foster (1862)

"Oh, Susannah," by Stephen Foster (1848)

"Big Deal," music by Harley White, Jr., words by Mark Stein

PROPERTY LIST

Vaudeville annunciator board and signs
White half-masks
Women's underwear (PROSECUTOR)
Briefcase (BRODSKY)
Business card (BRODSKY)
Candy bar (BRODSKY)
Silk handkerchiefs (BRODSKY)
Coat (BRODSKY)
Soviet flag (BRODSKY)
Contract (BRODSKY, WHITE)
Pen or pencil (BRODSKY, WHITE)
Newspaper (OLEN)
Playing cards (CHARLIE, ANDY, EUGENE, LEROY)
Curtain rod with center-slit curtain attached (TWO BOYS)
Guitar (OZIE)
Broom (CLARENCE)
Piece of paper (WILLIE)
Straw hats and canes (LEIBOWITZ AND KNIGHT)
Purse (VICTORIA)
Watch (VICTORIA)
Pin (VICTORIA)
Dutch (small sharpened object) (HAYWOOD)